CW00621321

Meeting God
Through Worship

Meeting God Through Worship

Anne Broyles

Abingdon Press
Nashville

MEETING GOD THROUGH WORSHIP

Copyright © 1992 by Abingdon Press

All rights reserved.
No part of this work may be reproduced or transmitted in any form or by any means, electronic or mechanical, including photocopying and recording, or by any information storage or retrieval system, except as may be expressly permitted by the 1976 Copyright Act or in writing from the publisher. Requests for permission should be addressed in writing to Abingdon Press, 201 Eighth Avenue South, Nashville, TN 37203.

This book is printed on acid-free, recycled paper.

Library of Congress Cataloging-in-Publication Data

Broyles, Anne, 1953–
   Meeting God through worship / Anne Broyles.
     p. cm.—(Vital signs series)
   Includes bibliographical references.
   ISBN 0-687-24655-5 (alk. paper)
   1. Public worship. I. Title. II. Series.
BV176.B76   1992
264—dc20   92-333

Scripture quotations, unless otherwise noted, are from the New Revised Standard Version of the Bible, copyright © 1989 by the Division of Christian Education of the National Council of Churches of Christ in the USA. Used by permission.

Scripture quotations marked GNB are from the *Good News Bible*—Old Testament: Copyright © American Bible Society 1976; New Testament: Copyright © American Bible Society 1966, 1971, 1976.

Quotations marked BSE are from the *Five Week Psalter*, © 1985 by the Benedictine Sisters of Erie, Inc., 6101 East Lake Rd., Erie, Pennsylvania 16511

Scripture quotations marked ILL are from *An Inclusive Language Lectionary*, copyright © by the Division of Education and Ministry, National Council of Churches in the USA; Year A © 1986, Year B © 1987, Year C © 1988.

Scripture paraphrases marked AP are the author's paraphrase of the Bible.

Quotations from *Touch Holiness*, copyright © 1990 are reprinted with permission of Pilgrim Press. All rights reserved.

MANUFACTURED IN THE UNITED STATES OF AMERICA

To the people of Christ United Methodist Church,
Norwalk, California (1951 – 1991)

CONTENTS

Vital Signs. What does that mean? In the context of the human body, vital signs are marks of health and life—pulse rate, blood pressure, body temperature. What might *vital signs* mean for the church?

Vital signs in the life of the Body of Christ consist of features of congregational life that define and measure its health, its vigor. Such signs include prayer, study, outreach, and worship. These signs are found on several levels. The spiritual life of each member contributes to the spirituality of the entire congregation. Group study, especially Bible study, enriches the congregation in knowledge and understanding. Outreach binds individuals in a common purpose. Worship tailored to private and corporate meditation and praise yields a sense of authentic community before God.

The Vital Signs books have been created to help the people of God register vital signs of life for service to one another and to God who "made us alive together with Christ" (Eph. 2:5). To that end this series is dedicated.

On Sunday morning, volunteers set up folding chairs in the high school gym, preparing for worship. Peter Johnson and Brett Gilian carefully move in the table that will serve as communion table and altar. Mary Bottoms then covers it with her best tablecloth and places two candlesticks and a bouquet of flowers cut from her garden. Rob and Julie Kizac arrive and plug in the sound equipment, ready for their folk music group to open the service with "You Are My Hiding Place." Within minutes, the gym has been transformed from a place to play basketball to a sanctuary of Christian worship.

Miles away, in a large sanctuary noted for its huge pipe organ and striking stained-glass windows, Mildred Banner changes the silk paraments from white to red. Andrea and Sarah Chun move their youth group banner around the front of the church, trying to place the dove and flames design so everyone can see it. The florist delivers the altar floral arrangement and stops for a minute to listen to the sixty-member adult choir practice *"Veni Creator Spiritus"* ("Come, Creator Spirit").

In a small village in southern Africa, the congregation

gathers to celebrate the birthday of the church, despite the fact that it is not their turn on the circuit to have the pastor this week. In fact, it will be months until their minister once again visits their village. Nevertheless, church members know to wear red on this festive day, and when Mgbe Naramba begins singing *"Nyohene"* ("Come, Spirit Friend") many voices join joyfully.

It is Pentecost Sunday, and around the world, people of Jesus Christ gather to praise God and worship together. The setting and style of worship differ dramatically from place to place. Those worshiping include young and old, a wide variety of ethnicities and languages, people who have long been steeped in the faith, and those who are new to a life in Jesus Christ.

On the first Pentecost, the believers "were all together in one place" when they experienced the coming of the Holy Spirit. And, though they spoke many different languages, those believers were bound together in the one voice of God's Spirit. Today, the believers are scattered worldwide but still, whatever their vernacular of speech, the people of God understand the language of the heart, the Good News of salvation through Jesus Christ.

Whether a church is large enough to support a variety of program ministries or whether it is four families in a house church who come together for praise, worship is often both the core of life together and the main entry point into a church for most new people.

Why is worship so important to our life together? What exactly *is* worship? What are some of the different styles and modes of worship in contemporary congregations? What is the difference between individual and corporate worship? Do we need both? How does worship encourage Christians to live more faithfully? In what ways does worship help build Christian community?

Those of us who worship regularly do so for a variety of

reasons. As we prepare ourselves for Sunday morning worship or a Wednesday evening prayer service, it is unlikely that we consider questions such as those above. But exploring worship can help us learn about ourselves, one another, and God.

Meeting God Through Worship will look at worship in a way that is instructive, interpretive, and presents possibilities for individual spiritual growth as well as ideas for congregations seeking vital worship experiences. For both the church professional and the lay church member, this book offers an opportunity to grow closer to God as you use the questions at the end of each chapter for your personal meditation. So, in reading this book, you may want to read one chapter at a time, leaving a few minutes for reflection when you finish each chapter.

This book could be used in a group study by a local church worship committee, a women's or men's group, or a youth fellowship. *Meeting God Through Worship* could be the basis of a church staff retreat or part of a confirmation program.

The chapters of this book roughly follow an order of worship, beginning with our individual need to worship (chapter one), the need for corporate worship (two), the gathering (three), confession (four), Scripture and preaching (five), Holy Communion (six), and the sending forth (seven).

What is in this book is not as important as what it stimulates in *you* as you read it. Will you find a new way of preparing yourself for regular corporate worship? Will you try to schedule moments of personal devotion? Will you feel more connected to the people of God who gather to worship all around the world in the name of Jesus Christ?

It is my hope that you will not simply read this book and file it on the shelf in the appropriate category. Rather, my prayer is that each of you who reads *Meeting God Through Worship* will find here a word of comfort or challenge, an idea you wish to share with a friend, a quote that gives insight, some glimmer that leads you closer to God. Think of this as more of a process book (experiencing worship) than a how-to book.

In all of our studies, our discussions, our activities about worship, let us remember, as Paul reminded us in Romans 16:

> Let us give glory to God! [God] is able to make you stand firm in your faith, according to the Good News I preach about Jesus Christ. . . . To the only God, who alone is all-wise, be glory through Jesus Christ forever! Amen. (Romans 16:25*a*, 27 GNB)

Anne Broyles
Summer 1991
Malibu, California

Connecting to God

I know only enough of God to want to worship [God], by any means at hand.

Annie Dillard[1]

T he baby's arms wave excitedly, her body tilting to and fro in the backpack. The father looks around at his child, smiling at her enthusiasm.

"Just look quietly, Sarah. We don't want to scare the deer."

Across the clearing, the fawn stands, body tense, ready to run if necessary. Sensing no danger, the young deer dips its head down to munch on the tender grass at its feet. It raises its head only slightly when two other deer appear from the shadow of the bushes. The three stand in triptych, calmly eating a midmorning snack while the father and daughter watch in wonderment.

The baby's arms are still, her eyes wide as she stares at the deer.

"They're beautiful, aren't they, Sarah?" His whisper is reverential. "Gifts from God." And, standing in the presence of these enchanting creatures of the woods, both father and daughter respond to the wonder of God's creation.

For many of us, God's power clearly shows forth in the glories of nature. Quiet times, such as this father and daughter shared, enable us to connect to the power of a Creator God whose vast imagination includes swamps and storks, daffodils and dinosaurs, rivers, radishes, and rainbows.

A woman watching her children at play, a hiker surveying the world from the height of Mt. Denali, a grandmother savoring the first strawberries of summer, a visitor to an art museum who finds himself literally surrounded by Monet's *Water Lilies* panels—all share moments of awe, of feeling the tear in the eye, the lump in the throat at so much beauty, such perfection. In the deepest places within us, if not without, we fall to our knees in praise and thanksgiving at times like these.

Even the earliest humans realized that since they were unable to create natural wonders by their own power, there must be a greater-than-human Power whose creativity spawned the earth. There is a rich treasure of creation myths from virtually all early peoples. Where did we come from? Who made us? Why is the world the way it is? From the earliest times, people somehow knew that beauty is not an end in itself but represents creative power as well.

When we feel touched by the world's beauty or a friend's kindness, we realize that the God who gifted us with life continues to pour out on us blessing after blessing. For some, the beauty of creation most easily opens them to wonder at God's power. Others may feel the same need to worship when they hear a high school graduation speaker share her dreams for the world's future, attend an Amy Grant concert, or read a new and distinctive idea and remember that such creativity also comes from God.

When we come in touch with the Higher Power that is God, when we feel ourselves to be part of something bigger than our senses can understand, then we stand in awe, ready to worship.

Abraham Heschel wrote:

> Awe is an intuition for the dignity of all things, a realization that things not only are what they are but also stand, however remotely, for something supreme.
>
> Awe is a sense of the transcendence, for the reference everywhere to mystery beyond all things. It enables us to perceive in the world intimations of the divine, . . . to sense the ultimate in the common and the simple; to feel in the rush of the passing stillness the eternal. What we cannot comprehend by analysis, we become aware of in awe.[2]

In awe, we stand before God in our most natural state. We are empty of our need to stand out, to be seen, to make a statement. As we contemplate the wonder of the universe around us, we feel very insignificant. "I am filled with awe at the sight of the heavens, the sun, moon, and stars which you set in place. Who are we that you care for us?" (Psalm 8:3-4, BSE). Touched by the knowledge that God is more than we can ever comprehend, we are overwhelmed that this Creator God knows us and loves us, despite all we are.

In the busyness of our lives, we sometimes forget this incomprehensible love. We go about our daily tasks, living our individual routines until suddenly we come face to face with a reminder that God *is*, that God is with us, that God is in all the world. A tax consultant drives to her next appointment, concentrating on the details of her business and is suddenly confronted by a shimmering double rainbow off to the east. A waiter is wearily cleaning off a table when a customer comes over and says, "Thanks so much for your good service. God bless you." And his day is changed, the burdens on his shoulders are lighter now.

These moments of insight—God moments—remind us of our need to worship our Maker. Feeling a power beyond ourselves, we are ourselves more powerful. Awe seeps down into our very bones. Life is more than paying bills and carpooling to Little League practices and filing for Medicare. There is a level of meaning beyond what we most easily understand.

For those whose eyes are open, God's glory is all around us in factory towns as well as forests, in high-rise buildings as well as mountain heights. It may be harder to see God in the graffiti-covered subway walls or in the row of closed bankrupt shops in the depressed downtown, but Teilhard de Chardin once said that nothing on earth is profane for those who know how to see. On the contrary, everything is sacred.

Once we realize that all of life can offer opportunities for worship, we begin to see the holiness of our relationships, activities, thoughts, and deeds. The nightly story time with our children can be a time to meet God. Our morning run may now be a time to look for the sacred in the people and scenery we pass by. The preparation of a meal can be a time of thanksgiving for the fruits of the earth.

Moses, in encountering the burning bush, understood that all of life was sacred, holy ground. The God who spoke to him out of the bush continued an intimate relationship with Moses throughout his life. It is not any different for us. As songwriters Joe Elmore and Kay Mutert put it:

> Lord, this day and this place seem so
> ordinary. I've been here before:
> the same work to do, the same people
> I've been living with all along; there
> are no new shrubs in the yard. Is there

a fire I'm not seeing? Are you somewhere
here in all of this? Do you ever call my
    name?
Lord, however common it may appear, I'm
    going to name this day "sacred time,"
and this place "holy ground."[3]

Holy ground can be at any location. Sacred time can be at
any moment. In every place and time, there is always the
potential that we may meet God in a powerful way. God is
always ready to meet us; we are the ones who are distracted
enough at times that we miss the opportunities for those
divine encounters. One of the gifts of the Bible is that we have
numerous stories of ordinary people like ourselves who, much
to their surprise, met God and found their lives changed.

Samuel was sleeping in the sanctuary, a young boy serving
in the Temple under Eli, when God called him to be a
prophet. Mary was living the life of an ordinary village girl
when she discovered she was to be the mother of God.
Prominent in the government, a public servant named Isaiah
became a prophet when he experienced God through a
dramatic vision. When Rahab allowed two of Joshua's spies to
stay at her house, she did not know that she would soon risk
her own life that Joshua might take over Jericho. Ordinary
people throughout history have found their lives turned
upside down when they encountered the Living God.

We live ready to meet God when we are attentive to our
daily lives, expectant that we *will* meet the God of All Life.
Our ordinary experiences can be the means of knowing and
understanding God in new ways. Worship can be part of our
everyday lives.

In the seventeenth century, Brother Lawrence of the
Resurrection, a French Carmelite monk, developed a rich
spiritual life based on what he called "the practice of the

presence of God." This simply means remembering that God is with us in the present moment—always. Whether we are standing in line at the post office, washing dishes, making a hospital call, or feeling frustrated because the battery's gone out on our car, God is with us.

"The time of business is no different from the time of prayer," wrote Brother Lawrence. "In the noise and clatter of my kitchen, I possess God as tranquilly as if I were upon my knees before the Blessed Sacrament."[4] In other words, Brother Lawrence recognized that all of life was holy ground and sacred time.

We often meet God when we least expect it. Intent on a task or wrapped up in our own agenda, we are surprised by the epiphany of recognizing the presence of God. "Sometimes there's God, so quickly," says Blanche DuBois in *A Streetcar Named Desire*.[5]

Each of us can practice the presence of God, developing those spiritual disciplines that strengthen our awareness of the ways in which God works in our lives. Spiritual disciplines might include Bible study, prayer, silence and solitude, fasting, meditation, journaling, and individual worship. By choosing the disciplines that make the most sense for our particular lives, we increase our awareness of God's presence.

We don't have to be Brother Lawrence or Mother Teresa or one of the desert fathers and mothers. God meets us where we are, as *who* we are. So, if our lives include chicken pox, the presidential election, a Church Women United program, and the dog's rabies shot, that may be precisely where and how we meet God.

Most of us lead busy, active lives. Even if we prioritize time on Sunday morning for a corporate worship experience, we still need our own individual times of meeting God. This might happen spontaneously and unexpectedly, but we can also plan times for personal worship into our routine. An early morning walk can be a time of renewal. Or perhaps we would benefit from a nightly reading of the Psalms. One person may schedule moments each day to sit and watch the birds at her backyard feeder, understanding that she connects to God through their bright chirping. Another person may set a kitchen timer for ten minutes of silence each afternoon, sitting quietly in openness to what God may say.

Each person can carve out his or her own time to appreciate God's beautiful world, feel the unending grace of God, experience a depth of silence. Soaking in the power of God, we may feel renewed and recommitted in faith even if we had been feeling worn out, anxious, or depressed.

When we remain mindful of God's presence in all of life, each task that we undertake can take on a spiritual dimension. "This sums up our entire call and duty: to adore God and to love [God] without worrying about the rest," said Brother Lawrence.[6] Once we commit ourselves to worshipful living, tucking the kids in at night or dealing with personnel issues takes on a different dimension. Transformed by knowledge of God's power, we cope with the stresses of our ordinary lives differently.

I can remember traveling in Europe after I graduated from college. A French major, I thought I was pretty hot stuff, backpacking all over the Continent speaking only *en français.* After several months of this exciting life-style, I found myself in Nancy, France. The French were not fooled by my accent or my vocabulary. Friends I stayed with pointed out that one phrase I used (straight out of the dictionary, no doubt) would normally only be used by small children. Ego deflated, tired, and feeling a stranger in a strange land, I went for a walk and decided to go into a beautiful village church in Nancy.

Since the mass was in Latin (and unfamiliar to me, anyway), I sat during the worship service as if by myself. I did feel the strength of the gathered community, though, as their prayers and hymns surrounded me as I sat wearily in the pew. My mind was more on how my feet felt in my Lowa boots and how

far away from home I was than on anything as deep as God's
love or the Resurrection. It was late afternoon, and suddenly,
the sun streamed in through one wall's stained-glass windows,
illuminating the entire sanctuary as if by miracle. The change
within me was as dramatic as the transformation of that
sanctuary.

I sat up, no longer exhausted physically or mentally. My
eyes took in the splendor of those brilliant colors, watching
the light play around the formerly dim sanctuary. In that
moment, I felt God's presence so clearly and so vividly, I felt
empowered to continue the rest of my travels. Tired feet and
bruised ego no longer concerned me; God was with me.

We can be aware of God in all of life once we realize that our
lives are not compartmentalized into "God-moments" and
"the rest of life." Kahlil Gibran poignantly illustrated this in
"On Religion" from *The Prophet*:

> Who can separate his faith from his actions, or his belief from
> his occupations? Who can spread his hours before him, saying,
> "This for God and this for myself; This for my soul, and this
> other for my body?" . . . He to whom worshipping is a
> window, to open but also to shut, has not yet visited the house
> of his soul whose windows are from dawn to dawn. Your daily
> life is your temple and your religion. Whenever you enter into
> it take with you your all.[7]

Gibran reminds us that "the windows of our soul" are to be
open "from dawn to dawn." In work and in play, in joy and in
sorrow, when we feel like it and when we don't, worship can
come as naturally to us as breathing.

"Taste and see the goodness of God," the psalmist
encouraged us. Don't wait for Sunday worship or other
designated times to rendezvous with the Renewer of All
Things. Instead, expect to meet God in all of life.

Taste and see. God is in the way you work out differences

with your spouse; God is in the smell of creosote after rain; God is in you as you sink down into a warm bath. God stands ready to meet you at every moment in your life. Any moment can be a "God-moment," a call to worship. And any place can be a place of worship.

Questions for Reflection

— When have I been filled with awe of God?
— Are there places, events, or situations that consistently call forth in me a desire to worship God?
— In my daily routines, when am I most likely to meet God?
— When do I most feel connected to God?

Gathering with Other Believers

Companion of the lonely,
Binder of wounds,
Seeker of lost souls,
Friend of the poor,
Source of all that is,
Forgiver of sins,
Voice of the voiceless,
Counselor of the confused,
Shelter from the storm,
Creator of heaven and earth,
we in our ways worship and adore you.
Holly W. Whitcomb[1]

Esther is a committed Christian who makes time each morning to read a chapter or two from her Bible. "My days just start out better when I start with Scripture," she says. "I am calmer, at peace, ready to face whatever is to come." She smiles, thinking about her life. "But I also need my church service each Sunday. When I have to miss worship, it just doesn't feel right. Even when I'm on vacation,

I try to attend church wherever I am. It may not be *my* church, *my* community—but it's *church.*"

Worship is both a set time and place (Sunday at 11:00 A.M., for instance) and also ongoing (daily devotional times, other special services, whenever we experience God). When we worship, we celebrate God's presence in the world, reflecting on God, other people, our values, and all of life.

> Worship, in the broadest sense, is the approach of our hearts to God, the celebration of God's Word and acts. Everything that we do has the potential of being worship. . . .
>
> Worship, in a narrower sense, is a more structured, liturgical expression of the relationship between God—Creator and Redeemer—and us, the people of God.[2]

As important as private times of worship are in a Christian's life, corporate worship services fill a different need. We need times alone with God; we also need times with other worshipers, sharing an experience of faith that allows us to examine our lives in the perspective of heritage and hope.

Our faith is not lived out in a vacuum. Rather, we live as God's redeemed people in the midst of other human beings, all of whom are as needy (and as deserving) of God's love and forgiveness as we are. Because neither we nor those around us are perfect, we need to worship together with at least some of God's children in order that we may put into practice God's commandment to love one another. William Willimon defines worship as "the way we act out our love."[3]

First John 4:7, 16*b* reminds us, "Dear friends, let us love one another, because love comes from God. Whoever loves is a child of God and knows God . . . God is love, and whoever lives in love lives in union with God and God lives in union with that person" (GNB). In worship, we not only have a laboratory for love (even the most unified of worshiping congregations provides regular opportunities for tolerance, patience, and living out the fruits of the Spirit), we also join together as one to hear how this Loving God has worked throughout history for good in the world. We see in the example of Jesus Christ supreme love that extends beyond time, beyond place, beyond history.

Worship, then, gives us not only the chance to meet the God of Love in the depths of our own souls but also gives us the chance to act out our own love. As Quaker John Woolman wrote, "So far as true love influences our minds, so far we feel a desire to make use of every opportunity to lessen the distresses of the afflicted, and to increase the happiness of the creation . . . to turn all we possess into the channel of universal love becomes the business of our lives."[4]

Throughout the Bible and at the heart of our Judeo-Christian tradition is this mandate to love others, to give of ourselves. In coming closer to God through worship, we cannot help feeling called to share God's love, participating in that divine love that was so great that God was able to give Jesus Christ for the sins of the world. No matter what other realities we may experience in our world, the Love of God is the deepest reality out of which we live.

"Christian worship is the deliberate act of seeking to approach reality at its deepest level by becoming aware of God in and through Jesus Christ and by responding to this awareness," writes James White.[5] Obviously, worship involves more than sitting in a sanctuary for an hour each week. That service of worship (a designated time and place) is the prelude to the rest of life.

Corporate worship takes many forms. Even within a particular denomination, there is a great variety in style of worship. Some churches are highly liturgical, using a fixed order of worship that remains basically the same from week to week. Others may be less structured, adhering to a basic order with many variations depending on the church season and worship theme. There are other congregations who use no order of service but seek to respond to the Spirit of God as it moves in and among the worship leaders and congregation.

The form of worship, as varied as it may be, is not as important as the spirit in which we worship. "Worship is something Christians do communally in response to God," writes Don E. Saliers. "It is done not just from duty or obligation . . . but because it is the primary mode of remembering and expressing the Christian faith and the whole story of God in human history."[6]

Even in the earliest days of Christianity, the friends and followers of Jesus gathered together for worship. In celebration of the fact that Jesus had been resurrected and appeared to his disciples on that first Easter Sunday, early Christians met to give praise to the Powerful God who had raised Jesus from the tomb. Even earlier, documents from our Judeo-Christian tradition show, the people of God worshiped together each week. From around the sixth century B.C., the Hebrew people came together to read Scripture and sing psalms in praise of God. Certain people, most notably the Levites, were designated as priests with specific roles in worship as well as other functions.

Over the centuries, the role of clergy and laypeople has changed. There have been more and more opportunities for shared leadership in the church and in worship as well. Worship is not a performance done for the entertainment of those attending the service. Worship is a mutual corporate experience of all who gather together, whether they have leadership responsibilities or not.

Søren Kierkegaard presented an image of worship that has influenced many people since it was published more than one hundred years ago. Comparing worship to the theater, Kierkegaard wrote:

> In the theater, the play is staged before an audience who are called theatregoers; but at the devotional address, God is also

present. In the most earnest sense, God is the critical theatregoer, who looks on to see how the lines are spoken and how they are listened to: hence the audience is wanting. The speaker is then the prompter, and the listener stands openly before God. The listener, if I may say so, is the actor, who in all truth acts before God.[7]

This image opens us up to worship as a shared experience for which certain professionals (ministers, musicians) may be responsible for preparing but all who worship are responsible for participating. Church professionals are directors of the drama and, perhaps, the prompters. But everyone who enters the sanctuary ready to praise God is an actor for God, who is the audience.

"If we take the metaphor seriously and extend it to say that the Christian community through the ages is the playwright," adds David Owens,

> then congregational worship can be defined as a drama of the way the church perceives life to be, or a drama of the way life is lived when it is lived before God. . . . Worship is a drama that the church both creates and performs. It is the means through which the community of faith enacts again and again the story through which it receives its life.[8]

When we come prepared for worship, expecting to meet God, then we are able to more fully experience that designated time and place as "holy ground" and "sacred space." Rather than sitting back to hear what the preacher will say or how well the choir will sing, we join ourselves—body, mind, and spirit—to our community of faith. It is *our* worship; we are important to this drama; God awaits our response.

Liturgy—all that we say and do in worship—is indeed "the work of the people." There are no distinctions of "entertainer" and "audience" but rather, a community of individuals who play different roles as they actively participate in worship together.

When I was in high school, the only thing that kept me coming willingly to worship was the social network that I found in our choir and youth group. I rarely missed a Sunday, yet despite my singing in the choir, I was not an active participant in worship much of the time. The preacher (considered one of the finest in our area) was boring, I thought. The service was too static for me; my friends and I often sat in the choir loft, drawing messages to one another in the palms of our hands.

I was there, so I thought, only to be with my friends. Yet, even in the midst of that season of my life, I can clearly remember times when I happened to hear the preacher say something that made real sense or moments when I felt a lump in my throat as I sang a hymn. As hard as I tried to disassociate myself from the greater whole of worship at that church, God continued to come and meet me in ways that kept me coming to church and, indeed, led me to the ordained ministry. In worship, I knew myself to be somehow part of something greater than myself.

Since those high school days, I have attended numerous churches around the world. Some services of worship have moved me more than others, but I have come to realize that who *I* am and what I bring to worship (my inner preparation and state of mind) makes a great deal of difference in how I respond to any worship setting.

Most of us experience a variety of worship settings in our lives. We may grow up in one or more churches, attend a different worship service during young adulthood, and be part of other congregations as we move around during our adult lives. How does our experience of worship change as we find new communities with which to pray and sing and hear God's Word?

Each worshiping congregation is unique, even two

churches that share a common form of worship and happen to
choose the same hymns for a given Sunday. If we were to
attend two churches that, on the surface, were identical, we
would soon realize the uniqueness of each congregation. Each
congregation is composed of different people. Each has lived
through a different history. Each has its own thrust of mission
and ministry.

Ideally, an active worshiper would go to a new church and
have two thoughts, which may on the surface seem
antithetical:

"Wow! This is unlike any church I've ever attended. I like
the particular way they greet visitors (or do the children's
word or respond after the sermon);" *and* "I sure do feel at
home here."

In other words, each worshiping congregation should
express its own personality with worship that is authentic and
individual to a particular congregation at this moment in
history, even as it reflects elements that tie it firmly to
Judeo-Christian history and its own denominational affilia-
tion.

Worship that is vital and alive balances the strengths of its
faith tradition with the need to reflect the contemporary
situation. As church professionals and laypeople come
together as active participants, they share in a meeting with
God that is at the same time corporate and personal. Not
every hymn will touch every person. The sermon does not
affect any two people the same way. Worshipers even filter
their hearing of announcements, joys, and concerns through
their own experience.

Yet those who are open to God working in their midst will
usually find in each worship service some personal word from
God, which may be felt as simply as, "I need to be more
patient with Aunt Irvinia" or "Those words from 2 Corinthians
really spoke to me" or "Maybe I'm being too hard on

myself—God loves me anyway." This individual response to God comes in the midst of the corporate experience that may be expressed, "I felt so close to everyone at church today" or "It seems that God may be calling our church to open a soup kitchen."

Worship is a dialogue with God and those around us. We come each week as different people than we were the Sunday before. Some weeks we are more open to the new thing to which God may be calling us. There will be weeks when we can barely drag our weary selves to the sanctuary. Then, in the amalgam that happens any time the people of God gather to give praise to God's name, we are renewed and ready for action. There will be other weeks when we are able to reach out to a sister or brother who needs the love of Christ made real through human touch and voice.

But always, when we worship, God is among us. And there's no telling what may happen next.

Questions for Reflection

— What is my personal definition of worship?
— What have been some of my significant corporate worship experiences?
— When have I been most active as a participant in worship?
— What are some of the songs and scriptures that have been the most meaningful to me as I have worshiped?

Building Community

Come together, joining hands and hearts.
Let our hands be links of chain
which hold our lives together—
not a chain of bondage but a silver cord of
   strength,
a ribbon of love and faith and community,
giving us slack to sail the wind,
yet holding us in a mystical embrace,
that we may be alone but never lonely,
that we may be together but never lost in the crowd,
that we may be one without forfeiting uniqueness.
Come together, joining hands and hearts,
and let the spirit of God and the human spirit
flow in each one and through us all
as we gather here to share this time and space
and as we walk together on the journey.

                            John W. Howell[1]

Groups of people gather together for many reasons. Football games, rock concerts, political demonstrations, children's sports events, and parades all bring together a wide diversity of individuals in one place with a common purpose for that moment in time. Then, when the concert is finished or the parade has disbanded, those diverse individuals go their separate ways, no longer connected except by their individual memories of the experience. When the people of God gather, there may be just as wide a variety of people. They may gather in a cathedral or in the living room of a home, on any continent of the earth, at any time on any day. They may speak any language known to humankind or gather in silence.

But when the people of God gather, they gather in unity. When they leave their place of worship, they take with them not only the memory of that particular experience but the continuing relationship of being bound together in the spirit of Christ. The community of Jesus Christ is more than any one place or people. It is a synthesis of all those throughout history who have known Jesus as a reality in their lives.

We Christians have a common story that begins with God creating the earth and continues until the present moment. Scripture, hymns, historical writings on church doctrine and practice, and contemporary pronouncements on a variety of social issues are part of the fabric of our life together. Yet there are variations in how we interpret Scripture. Not all of us have read documents of our tradition from St. Augustine, Martin Luther, Teresa of Avila, or John Wesley. Not all Christians agree on nuclear disarmament, abortion, or gambling.

Unlike a country club, the church does not have requirements of social or economic standing. Unlike a political organization, the church requires no specific political belief system. For many of us, we come together in worship with people who are as *unlike* us as they are like us. So how is it that, in worship, we can come together in all our diversity and be one Body of Christ?

When my husband and I came as pastors to Malibu United

Methodist Church seven years ago, the chairperson of our staff-parish committee was a retired Marine Brigadier General, a veteran of three wars. My husband and I are known for our commitment to pacifism and nonviolence. In some ways, we had little in common with Duane. We probably do not vote the same way on many electoral issues. We may have different heroes. Our backgrounds, experiences, and certain values are worlds part. Because of that, there have been a few times when we have butted heads, vigorously discussing the sanctuary movement or the grape boycott. Always, when we have disagreed, we have sought to talk it out, to hear the others' viewpoint, to "agree to disagree" lovingly when needed. Why? Because the unity we feel in Christ is stronger than the differences between us.

"For now we see in a mirror, dimly, but then we will see face to face. Now I know only in part; then I will know fully, even as I have been fully known. And now faith, hope, and love abide, these three; and the greatest of these is love" (1 Corinthians 13:12-13). The love that Jesus Christ has shown to each of us binds us together in Christian community. Because we are part of Christ's church, Larry, Duane, and I have made an effort to listen to one another, to be present to one another, to share the love of Jesus. Despite the differences that may on the outside appear to be great, we have come to appreciate one another and value one another's opinions. The love and example of Jesus Christ helped us to know that we do not have to be the same as other people to truly love them.

When we were experiencing a conflict of opinions, celebrating World Communion Sunday, All Saints Day, or One Great Hour of Sharing reminded us of what was most important. Our differences could be laid aside as we participated in the gathering of Christ's people, the family of God.

One congregation found that thirty-five weeks of *Disciple*

Bible study just about tore their church apart. Because of the nature of that particular program of study, *Disciple* participants learned so much about one another, their differences were all too apparent.

"How can I remain in community with people who doubt my faith experience?" asked Delores Hart. "I have felt judged by some members of the Bible study, like I am not saved because I have come to God by a different path than they have."

This congregation was realizing the hard truth that Dietrich Bonhoeffer shared in his book *Life Together:*

> The serious Christian, set down for the first time in a Christian community, is likely to bring with him a very definite idea of what Christian life should be and try to realize it. But God's grace speedily shatters such dreams. Just as surely God desires to lead us to a knowledge of genuine Christian fellowship, so surely must we be overwhelmed by a great general disillusionment with others, with Christians in general, and, if we are fortunate, with ourselves. God is not a God of the emotions but the God of truth. Only that fellowship which faces such disillusionment . . . begins to be what it should in God's sight, begins to grasp in faith the promise that is given to it.[2]

Worship provided a healing opportunity for Bible-study members to once again feel Christ's unity. A small group worked with the pastor to plan a service around the theme, "Many Gifts, One Spirit." A footwashing and communion service brought them together again as they realized that "there are varieties of gifts, but the same Spirit; and there are varieties of services, but the same Lord. . . . To each is given the manifestation of the Spirit for the common good. . . . Now you are the body of Christ and individually members of it" (1 Corinthians 12:4-5, 7, 27).

From our different life experiences, we Christians gather

together in worship, opening ourselves to the miracle of unity that can happen when we focus on the power of Christ to transform us (rather than concentrating on the differences between us).

> So then, you Gentiles are not foreigners or strangers any longer; you are now fellow citizens with God's people and members of the family of God. You, too, are built upon the foundation laid by the apostles and prophets, the cornerstone being Christ Jesus himself. He is the one who holds the whole building together and makes it grow into a sacred temple dedicated to the Lord. In union with him you too are being built together with all the others into a place where God lives through God's Spirit. (Ephesians 2:19-22, GNB)

Paul uses the image of a building, with Christ as the cornerstone and all believers being built into "a sacred temple dedicated to the Lord." Henri Nouwen illustrates Christian community as "a large wagon wheel to make the point that the closer we come to God—the hub of our life—the closer we come to each other, even when we travel along very different paths (spokes)."[3]

Sheila Cassidy gives the cross as a model for our life together: the upright as our relationship to God, the crossbeam as our relationship with one another.[4] Others have compared the life of a Christian to that of a coal that cannot exist outside the fire. In order to retain heat, the coal must be in close proximity to the larger fire and other coals. Otherwise, its fire burns out. Likewise, it is said, we Christians need to gather together as the Body of Christ so that we continue to feel the flame of God's love and our commitment to spreading the good news of Jesus Christ.

"But," some say, "I don't need to go to church to feel close to God. And when I go to church, it's sometimes distracting for me. Babies crying, people to talk to, that cranky lady in the

pew in front of me. . . ." It may be easier to worship God
without having to deal with God's children, but for those of us
who do not live the life of a hermit, worship gives us practice
in living the life of love we are called to.

Even in the formational years of Christianity when there
were fewer Christians with whom to get along, Paul
repeatedly had to bring up the realities of how followers of
Christ could work together to form community. When Paul
wrote to the church at Ephesus, he encouraged them to

> be always humble, gentle, and patient. Show your love by
> being tolerant with one another. Do your best to preserve the
> unity which the Spirit gives by means of the peace that binds
> you together. There is one body and one Spirit, just as there is
> one hope to which God has called you. There is one Lord, one
> faith, one baptism; there is one God . . . who works through
> all, and is in all. (Ephesians 4:2-6, GNB)

Because we are baptized in Christ, we are family. We come
together to worship, to pray, to sing, to study, to play *as
family*. New church member Kwo Ka Pak says, "As a
Christian, I belong to the community. I am not Christian
alone. I am part of the body of Christ. That makes me feel
good. I *belong*."

Those who are baptized include the young, old, and
in-between; new immigrants and early settlers; people of
every shade and hue; those who speak in tongues and those
who don't; people who call themselves "liberal," "conservative," or "moderate," and those who eschew any label or
category. In short, the only sure thing the baptized have in
common is their baptism in Christ.

When the baptized come together to worship the God who
makes them family, they come as individuals, adding their
uniqueness to the unity of the corporate body. Author M.
Enid Watson puts it this way:

To worship is to listen for the ancient song of creation and to
recognize within that song our individual songs. To worship is
to share these melodies and dissonances of our human
condition. Our voices vary: some warble, some bellow, but the
song is universal. It is our ode to God, and to the God within
us.[5]

We may sing "Amazing Grace" in German, Cherokee, or
Tagalog. We may sing alto, tenor, bass, or soprano. We may
have all the verses memorized or need to look at a hymnal.
But, with hearts and voices, we gather together to praise the
God whose powerful actions in history and our own lives have
convinced us to throw our lot in with God's son, Jesus Christ.

Baptism is our initiation into the Body of Christ. When the
community of faith participates in a baptism during worship,
all who gather there welcome the newly baptized into the
family. We celebrate the love of God that reaches out to all
people whether they are newborn or aged. And we give
thanks for the symbol of water that reminds us of the new life
all Christians have in Christ.

We need symbols as tangible reminders of what God is
doing in our lives. Hearing the water poured into the
baptismal font, we can remember times when we have felt
clean and refreshed by such an ordinary gift which, in the
symbolic act of baptism, becomes extraordinary.

Baptism is not the only reminder that God is with us.
Funerals, weddings, baptismal renewals, confirmation, and
communion are all important rituals that help us feel close to
God and one another. "Rituals are a community's repeated
symbolic actions expressing its memory and vision," writes
John H. Westerhoff III. "Rituals are at the center of human
life, binding together past, present, and future. . . . Rituals
are repetitive symbolic actions that express a community's
myth or sacred story."[6]

One congregation always gathers at the front of the

sanctuary for infant and toddler baptism, crowding close to watch the ritual. They sing, "He's Got the Whole World in His Hands" as the minister carries the child from person to person so each can give a personal blessing to the new family member. Another church's members look forward to the annual baptismal renewal service, when each person comes forward to receive water from the baptismal font in the sign of a cross on the forehead.

From church to church, congregations find ways to personalize Christian rituals in their own context. The ways of serving communion or receiving new members help define who that community of faith is. Rituals are not only connectors to the past but also statements of identity in the present.

All of our worship rituals retell our common story as the people of God. The sacrament of Baptism, for instance, reminds us of Jesus who was himself baptized by water and the spirit. We feel connected to those New Testament brothers and sisters who were baptized and, indeed, know ourselves to be related to all baptized persons throughout history.

The sacrament of Holy Communion reminds us of the Jesus who sat at table with close friends, promised them his Spirit, and returned to them after his earthly death. Like those friends who knew him well, we know ourselves to be recipients of that sustaining and enabling Spirit.

Rituals help us mark and understand our passages through various life-stages. Confirmation signifies a young person's readiness to take on the life of Christ in greater understanding and responsibility. When we gather to witness a wedding, all present know that the marriage couple is taking a significant step in their mutual life journey. A funeral helps us celebrate the life of the person who has died and also reminds us of our own mortality and the promise of eternal life.

All of these rituals take place within the context of community. When a youth is confirmed or baptismal vows are renewed, all of us think of our own baptism and the vows we have made to serve Christ within his church. When a couple stands before the community to declare their love, each of us gives thanks for the love and commitment that can exist between two lovers. When we gather at a funeral, we look backward to the life of the person who has died and also forward to our own death and resurrection.

Rituals bind us together as we celebrate God's love as it has been made known to us throughout history and in our own lives, through personal experience or the experience of the community. Even if I am not married, I can understand the depth of the promises made by a wedding couple. Even if I have never been confirmed, I can give thanks for the faith of the young person standing before the congregation ready to say yes to Christ's call. Though I am still alive, I contemplate the mystery of death.

When we gather for worship, we come with our individual needs to praise, to give thanks, to witness to what God is doing in our lives. We also come to build community with one another, to share ourselves in our strength and our vulnerability, our faith and our doubting, our joys and our sorrows. In the corporate sharing of worship, we are made one in Christ. This does not mean that we will be intimate friends with everyone in our worshiping community. It does not mean that we will always agree with our neighbor in the pew or the minister in the pulpit. But as we sing and pray together, our individual voices join together to be more than we are separately.

When we gather with the same worshiping community on a regular basis, we begin to know one another as family. Even if we do not know the name of that gray-haired man who each Sunday walks slowly to the front of the sanctuary with his cane, we recognize him as the gentle soul he is, as sort of a beneficent uncle. The little red-haired girl who loves to twirl in circles in the aisle during hymn-singing feels like a niece or cousin. Likewise, the person we neither like nor appreciate is also related to us. All of these people, because we share the worship experience and know God's presence to be among us, become a collection of relatives—some close, some distant, all family.

As we gather together with other persons of faith, we bring our private fears and frustrations about life and, hearing the power of God proclaimed, begin to make sense out of our lives. There are times when we need to be alone with God, focusing on how God's immense love has an impact on our lives. Other times, we need to gather with the people of God, "for where two or three are gathered in my name," Jesus told us, "I am there among them." Bound together in the love of God through Christ Jesus, we are one family, a community of believers. And whether we worship in a congregation of thirty or a thousand, we are at home, surrounded by aunts and uncles, nieces and nephews, cousins and grandparents, sisters and brothers.

This feeling can exist even when we worship with a faith community that is unfamiliar to us. There is in any Christian community that Spirit of Christ that transcends the barriers that might otherwise divide us. Obviously, there are some communities that will feel more comfortable for our particular journey. For those of us who are accustomed to a small worshiping community, a large sanctuary with four hundred worshipers may feel overwhelming. If inclusive language is important to us, then we may feel alienated in a worship service that uses all male pronouns for God and humanity. If we do not usually worship in a charismatic community, with speaking in tongues, we may have to remind ourselves that all movements of and responses to the Spirit can be valid, even if we do not feel comfortable in a particular context.

Our baptism in Christ binds us together even when our methods of worship differ. Being in unity does not mean being the *same*. Jesus, on the night before he was crucified, prayed fervently to God, "The glory that you have given me I have given them, so that they may be one, as we are one, I in them and you in me, that they may be completely one, so that the world may know that you have sent me and loved me and have loved them even as you have loved me" (John 17:22-23).

This love of Jesus can help us look for those elements that could bind us to an unfamiliar worshiping community rather than dwelling on the differences between us. In this age of "church shopping," people take more opportunity to search for their ideal faith community—the church they feel will meet their needs. Sometimes, however, we may find more personal growth if we seek out a faith community that brings new dimensions of the Christian life to our experience.

When we worship with people who are a mixture of ages, ethnicities, economic backgrounds, and theological perspectives, we open ourselves to new learnings about God and our own faith. No one faith experience is the norm. The more we celebrate the diversities among us, the greater will be our experience of Christ's unity.

One of my most meaningful worship experiences came when I was traveling in Sierra Leone. The church was up a bumpy dirt road in the midst of simple homes. The people who gathered spoke a variety of languages. Their spirit was obviously focused on the gracious God who had brought them together. I have rarely experienced such a high level of energy in worship; although the service lasted more than two and a half hours, not even our twenty-two month old daughter became restless.

Those seated in the congregation gave lively verbal response to much of what the pastors said, eager to add their own enthusiasm. When it was time for the collection, one of the ministers told how much *he* was giving to the common plate and then invited men and women to come forward to place their offerings in separate plates. "Who will give the

most?" he teased. "Women or men?" And, looking out at the
congregation, he pointed to individuals: "Brother, can't you
come up here to put in a large amount?" "Sister, surely you
won't miss this opportunity to give to God?" Smiles on their
faces, tithes and offerings in their hands, members of the
congregation came up one at a time, joyous as they put their
gifts for God's work into the offering plate.

When the collection was finished, the choir sang a rendition
of "In the Garden." Though this has never been one of my
favorite hymns, I was touched by the fact that they dedicated
this music to the earlier Evangelical United Brethren
missionaries who had introduced it to them. The liveliness of
their worship was due in part to the multilingual music of the
congregation; they were in touch, though, with the English-
speaking church workers who had been one of the ways God
came to them.

I could not understand the language of much of the worship
service. But that was unimportant. This congregation's obvious
love of God and one another welcomed me into their family.

"There is none like you among the gods, O Lord, nor are
there any works like yours. All the nations you have made
shall come and bow down before you, O Lord, and shall
glorify your name" (Psalm 86:8-9). When we gather with other
believers, whether they live in Cairo or Quito, speak Malay or
Swedish or Hebrew, we gather as community. We gather to
glorify God's name and tell of the great things God has done
throughout the earth and, yes, even in our own lives. One
family of God, we know ourselves to be at home wherever the
people of God gather.

Questions for Reflection

— What have been some of my special times of feeling a
  sense of community in worship?

— Are there particular individuals in my congregation that feel like family to me?

— When, in a community of faith, has someone else's sharing of their faith journey helped me understand my own life of faith in a new way? Am I open to such sharing with persons whose experiences and commitments may be different than my own?

— What are helpful images for me when I consider the corporate dimensions of worship: a wagon wheel, a building, the cross, the coal within the fire, other images?

Understanding Our Place in God's World

Worship is a way of seeing the world in the Light of God.   Abraham Heschel[1]

The Hebrew people grew into their identity as the people of God. Although they had previously shared life as an ethnic group oppressed under the pharoah's rule, it was not until they sojourned for forty years in the desert that they keenly felt their kinship with one another as God's Chosen People. Having been liberated from slavery, led to the Promised Land, the people of Israel were a community, bound in covenant to God.

In Deuteronomy 7, Moses reminded the Israelites:

For you are a people holy to Yahweh your God; Yahweh has chosen you out of all the peoples on the earth to be God's people, God's treasured possession. It was not because you were more numerous than any other people that Yahweh's heart was set on you—for you were the fewest of all peoples. It was because Yahweh loved you and kept the oath sworn to your ancestors, that Yahweh has brought you out with a mighty hand and redeemed you from the house of slavery,

from the hand of Pharaoh king of Egypt. Know therefore that
Yahweh is God, the faithful God who maintains covenant
loyalty with those who love Yahweh and keep Yahweh's
commandments, to a thousand generations. (Deuteronomy
7:6-9 AP)

Understanding their relationship to God in terms of both
their history and their future, the Hebrew people knew their
place in the world. They knew who and Whose they were. As
Jacob set up a memorial stone at Bethel, designating it as a
place to worship God, the Israelites stopped along the way to
feel at home, to remind themselves *why* they were moving
and *Who* was leading them. They followed intricate
procedures to set up a Tent of the Lord's Presence at each of
the places they stayed.

When they were finally ready to cross into the land of
Canaan, Joshua instructed God's Chosen People to set up
twelve stones, both in the middle of the Jordan River and at
Gilgal, "for the LORD your God dried up the waters of the
Jordan for you until you crossed over, so that all the peoples of
the earth may know that the hand of the LORD is mighty, and so
that you may fear the LORD your God forever" (Joshua
4:23-24).

The Hebrew people knew their special relationship to God
through the desert journey, the traveling Tent of the Lord's
Presence, and the rock monuments. For most of *us*, worship
is the binding experience that helps each of us know who and
Whose *we* are in the context of Christian community. In
worship, we can begin to make sense of our lives in particular
and our world in general. Just as the Hebrew people needed
the Tent of God's Presence and other reminders, we need
private and corporate worship experiences to help us
remember the God who loves us and journeys with us.

"We come to the church," says John Westerhoff

not because we have faith but because we desire it and know it can be ours only if we live in a community of faith. We come to the church not because we understand scripture but because we want to, and because we know that if we are to understand, we will need the help of the community which made it holy. In the experience of Christ at baptism, in [communion and other community worship events], and in other sacraments, Christians come to know the Christ of scripture and are thereby enabled to make sense of the Gospels.[2]

When we gather to worship, we are able to celebrate the joys in our lives, to lift up the areas of concern, and to be honest about the ways we have fallen short of our call to follow Christ. Part of our "making sense of the Gospels" is the time of confession when we look at our daily lives in the light of the example of Jesus. Have we always been loving? unselfish? patient?

As part of a study on how parents' handling of conflict influences children's self-esteem, my husband, daughter, and I filled out daily forms of detailed questions about our interaction with one another. Each night for six weeks we rated our interactions on a scale of 1 to 5. We responded to such statements as "I showed love to my child today," "I disregarded my spouse's feelings," and "I nagged/yelled at/punished/didn't have time for my child." Even on the best, most stress-free days, when I filled out the questionnaire, I had moments of wishing I had shown *more* love or nagged less or had taken more time to simply *be* with my family.

The study's questionnaire was not designed to make any of us feel guilty or inadequate about our family relationships but rather to help psychologists determine factors in family life that promote healthy self-esteem in American children. The benefit of the study for our family was the daily time of reflection in which each of us could prayerfully evaluate our day, considering the ways we could be *more* loving and supportive with one another the next day.

In worship, confession provides a similar time of reflection. We look realistically at our lives, not to wallow in our abject sinfulness but to take honest stock of who we are and then to be encouraged toward more Christlike behaviors.

On a personal level, we think of ways we can be more authentically Christian as we interact with family, neighbors, and co-workers. "Search me, O God, and know my heart; test me and know my thoughts. See if there is any wicked way in me, and lead me in the way everlasting" (Psalm 139:23-24). On a community level, we realize some of the ways our congregation may not be following God's call; we seek to look at our nation's actions as well, in the light of God's will. "God . . . will judge the world with righteousness, and the peoples with God's truth" (Psalm 96:13*b*, ILL).

Most of us are uncomfortable when we think about sin, whether it be our personal failings or those of a community or nation. There are so many things we do *right,* why should we dwell on those things that are negative in our lives? We are not ax-murderers, embezzlers, robbers in the night. We are simply ordinary human beings who don't always act in the ways we should.

However, sin is more than any one action or thought. Sin, as Tillich reminded us, is a state of separation from ourselves, from one another, from God. "To be in a state of sin," writes David Owen, "is to self-righteously . . . experience yourself, the neighbor and the very fabric of life as fundamentally warped, misdirected, askew. To be in a state of sin is to be in a state of defiance toward ourselves, our neighbor or life as it is given to us day by day."[3]

Confession, then, takes into account this condition of sinfulness—being separated from ourselves, from one another, from God—as much as reckoning the individual ways we act out our separation. When I wish to be other than my real self, I am separated from self. When I do not accept my neighbor as who he or she is, I am separated from sister or brother. When I do not live out the oneness with God that is my gift, I am separated from God.

Although I would rather not have to consider this state of separation, I realize that by honestly appraising my life in its sinfulness, I am freed to live into the future, unbound by the past. Rather than holding on to patterns that keep me from living in the fullness of God's new life, I can confess who I am, ask for pardon, and receive the forgiveness that God jubilantly wants to give me.

We are able to honestly confess before the God who loves us and works in us, knowing that "indeed, God did not send the Son into the world to condemn the world, but in order that the world might be saved through him" (John 3:17). We are able to confess in the midst of community because we are all on the same path, seeking to come closer to God. Though some among us seem to be more consistently Christlike, all of us are human, prone to the self-centered myopia that results in our acting out from our own understanding, rather than from the broader worldview that faith in God can give.

> Therefore, my friends . . . let us approach with a true heart in full assurance of faith, with our hearts sprinkled clean from an evil conscience and our bodies washed with pure water. Let us hold fast to the confession of our hope without wavering, for he who promised is faithful. And let us consider how to provoke one another to love and good deeds, not neglecting to meet together . . . but encouraging one another. (Hebrews 10:19a, 22-25a)

Whenever a small group gathers in a church, be it a men's fellowship, a church women's organization, or a young mothers' support group, there can be sharing that encourages the best from each participant. Many people know how hard it is to act out one's faith in the professional world, and so crave examples of Christian peers who are able to define *success* in a way that includes fidelity to one's faith. Church women's organizations carefully study world situations to see what the most effective mission and outreach might be, given the reality of their lives. Most young mothers have times of losing patience with a toddler and can benefit from tactics that have worked in other households. In our sharing, praying, studying together, confession can take place informally.

Confession in a formal worship setting usually comes in the form of a printed prayer of confession and, often, silent meditation. Though the printed words may not necessarily apply to our particular situation as we review our lives, we pray with the community, knowing that there are many ways in our own lives that we need to come closer to God. In praising the God of Love, we realize how we have betrayed that love.

And God's love is what makes all the difference. We are not standing with head hung low before a wrathful parent who will cruelly punish us for our wrongdoing; we stand before a God of Love who, in receiving our confession, releases us to "go and sin no more." We know who we are (mortals in need of that second chance) and Whose we are (children of a Loving Savior).

So, baptized in Christ, we are given a unique perspective on our world. We know that we do not always live up to our baptismal vows. But we also live with the knowledge that a God of Love is in charge of the world. Reading the headlines of newspapers and magazines, we realize that these communications do not tell the entire story. Yes, there is war, famine, unbelievable violence in our world. But there is also generosity, peacemaking, numerous "good Samaritans" whose acts do not make the public press.

In the movie *Awakenings* a new drug therapy brings a middle-aged man "alive" again after thirty years in a coma. As Leonard adjusts to new life in a different world, he is filled with joy and one day calls his doctor at 5:00 A.M. with "important news":

> We've got to tell everybody. We've got to remind them how good it is. Read the newspaper and what does it say? All bad. It's all bad. People have forgotten what life is all about. They've forgotten what it is to be alive. They need to be reminded about what they have and what they can lose and what I feel is the joy of life, the gift of life, the freedom of life, the wonderment of life.[4]

Isn't that a part of our task as Christians? We can be that reminder of the gift of life in all its fullness. Confession involves not only our acknowledgment of personal sin but also confessing our faith that God is active in the world in ways we may not see or understand. Even in the midst of awful situations, a promise exists: Jesus, dying on the cross, turned to the criminal hanging next to him and said, "Truly I tell you, today you will be with me in Paradise" (Luke 23:43).

This is not a "pie-in-the-sky" philosophy, standing outside reality, living for the future but unable to cope with present realities. Rather, we live today in confidence that the world as we know it is not the total reality. Kenneth Bedell says,

> The Christian gospel presents a message which cuts through tension, pressure, and frustration, not by denying reality but rather by putting reality into perspective. True worship makes us feel good not because we have avoided reality but because we have participated in and come to understand reality at its deepest level.[5]

As individuals, we find a variety of ways to express this hope. Archbishop Desmond Tutu has continued to speak out against apartheid even through the years when South African racism seemed most firmly entrenched. Elizabeth McAlister and Phil Berrigan have been arrested numerous times in protest against the nuclear arms buildup in the United States. Concerned with the plight of American children, Marian Wright Edelman founded the Children's Defense Fund. Other persons join prayer groups, write letters, visit nursing homes, or build senior citizen housing.

Congregations find their own ways of acting out their faith as well. One congregation may show its solidarity with the undocumented workers in their area by providing legal assistance and English classes. Another congregation may stand against homophobia by declaring itself as a safe and welcoming place for gay and lesbian people. In rural communities, congregations may respond to the farm crisis and farmers' needs by caring for families whose farms must be auctioned or by forming tractor brigades to state representatives' offices. Each individual, each congregation, confesses its faith in ways appropriate to its unique situation.

No matter what the prevailing reality may seem to be, we know who and Whose we are, and that makes all the difference. Because "by God's great mercy we have been born anew to a living hope through the resurrection of Jesus Christ from the dead, and to an inheritance which is imperishable, undefiled, and unfading, kept in heaven for you, who by God's power are guarded through faith for a salvation ready to be revealed in the last time" (1 Peter 1:3b-5 AP).

Questions for Reflection

— How do I view the world differently because I believe in God?

— How would I describe God's role in my life? in the world?

— When am I most sure of *who* and *Whose* I am?

— What are the hardest sins for me to confess?

Living into the Word of God

We give thanks, O God of sacred stories, for the witness of holy scripture. Through it, you nurture our imaginations, touch our feelings, increase our awareness, and challenge our assumptions. Bless, we pray, our hearing of your word this day. Speak to each of us; speak to all of us; and grant that by the power of your Spirit, we may be hearers and doers of your word.

Ann B. Day[1]

L ast April, as he calmly sat at the ten o'clock worship service, Harry James found himself leaning forward in the pew, straining to hear what the lay liturgist was reading from Luke 9. Oh, he'd heard these words about the would-be followers of Jesus before. Harry had always been sympathetic to the plight of those who wanted to follow Jesus but couldn't just then, for one reason or another. But that April day, Jesus' words struck him anew: "No one who puts a hand to the plow and looks back is fit for the Reign of God."

These words were still rumbling around inside him when the minister read from 1 Timothy 6. This passage, too, was familiar—beware of riches and all that. Only now, Harry felt the weight of the words, because just this week Jerry Kawashima had called, inviting Harry to spend his vacation with Habitat for Humanity. "Sounds great," Harry had replied. "But Doris and I already have plans for a Caribbean cruise." As he hung up the phone, Harry had been painfully aware of his priorities. A building contractor, he had important skills for a Habitat project of building homes for the needy. But surely all his hard work over the years deserved the reward of a luxury cruise. Now, hearing these scriptures, Harry made a decision: He would at least talk to Doris. Maybe working with Habitat could fit into their plans somehow.

Harry, like many of us, enjoyed the familiarity of Sunday worship's Scripture lessons. Over a lifetime in the church, he felt as if he knew the Bible fairly well. But there it was—familiar scripture had once again come to him in a new way, forcing him to look at the reality of his life and grow into new understandings of himself as a follower of Jesus.

Worship not only brings God's Word alive but helps us live into the call of that Word. Scripture reading is not something we do simply to connect with the long Christian tradition. God's Word comes to us fresh, pinpointed to our own life and situation. William Willimon writes:

> To listen to scripture is to be confronted with a vision of a new heaven and a new earth. It is to be given, as it were, new lenses through which we see a very different kind of world. Our vision becomes dull. We eventually see only what we want to see, only what we think is possible, permissible. When we open the scriptures, our world view is cracked open, the mists clear, and we see things in a new way.[2]

Whether we study the Bible on our own or hear it proclaimed in worship, we cannot help being struck by how aptly the words of Scripture can speak as if meant for us alone. Words echo from the hills of Judea to our part of Boston or Chattanooga or Billings. We hear and respond with the same energy as those who heard Jesus' voice long ago.

When Philip heard the Ethiopian eunuch reading from Isaiah, he asked him, "Do you understand what you are reading?" The Ethiopian replied, "How can I, unless someone guides me?" And, when Philip began to interpret the scripture, the Ethiopian energetically said, "Look, here is water! What is to prevent me from being baptized?" (Acts 8:26-38). The eunuch heard the scripture, understood its meaning, and was ready to commit himself to Jesus Christ.

Most of us can benefit from guidance as we read the Bible. We may learn from one another in a group Bible study; we may receive new insights on a passage of Scripture as the minister preaches during worship. As much as we need personal times of Bible study, we sometimes hear God's Word differently when it comes to us in community. What a rich experience it can be to share with other believers, to recognize again that God's Word comes to us in ways unique to our own lives.

In a midweek Bible study, for instance, six women gather to study Scripture together. A new Christian, Beth is making a new start in her life after several years of drug and alcohol abuse. Beth is constantly amazed at the nonjudgmental way in which Jesus speaks to her, offering new life. Mabel is a staunch churchgoer and has been in one Bible study or another for more than sixty years; now that she is in her senior years, she finds herself turning for comfort to different Scripture passages than she had earlier in life. Kathleen has recently returned to church after experimenting with Eastern religions. "The Bible really has a unique perspective," she says, "even though I see similarities to other traditions." Geneva comes from the South and often quotes her beloved grandmother who made Scripture come alive for her. Yasmin is trying to learn about Christianity, her husband's faith, and finds many similarities between it and her birth religion of Islam. Marty is a college junior, searching for answers to important questions about life and love.

When these women gather, they read the same Scripture passages. But because of their different life experiences, the Bible speaks to each individually. Their common study illuminates the many applications each Bible verse could have as it speaks to different persons. Likewise, the women read out of different translations of the Bible and find that comparing Beth's *New International Version*, Kathleen's *New Revised Standard Version*, Marty's *Good News Bible*, and Mabel's *King James Version*, they become aware of nuances of meaning not as evident in any one translation. Geneva brings her *Living Bible*, a paraphrase of Scripture, not an actual translation, which often makes the meaning plain for contemporary life.

The women in this Bible study realize that the Bible helps us rehearse our history as the people of God, reminding us of the many ways God has been continuously working in human history. Reading Hebrews 11, for instance, we are amazed at the faith held by Abel, Enoch, Noah, Abraham, Isaac, Jacob, Sarah, Moses, the Hebrew people, Rahab, and many others. "Now faith is the assurance of things hoped for, the conviction of things not seen," we are told, and recounting the lives of those faithful who have gone before us, we are ready to look at our own lives. In what ways are we living that life of "the assurance of things hoped for, the conviction of things not seen"? How do we show thanks for "so great a cloud of witnesses"?

Each Scripture passage, whether heard in worship or read alone, offers us the chance to connect with our history as God's people, to look at our present lives, and to dedicate ourselves to a future as God's people in this world. As Don Saliers writes:

Without living remembrance of the whole biblical story there would be no authentic worship, nor could there be such a thing as becoming a living reminder of Jesus Christ for others. Seeking God and embodying holiness in our whole existence is, in great measure, a matter of receiving and exercising the memories of the Scriptures in and through particular forms of communal traditions. Living our lives open to God requires dwelling in a common history, the teachings, the writings of the prophets, the witness of the apostles, and the extended memories of the community praying and living in accordance with them through time.[3]

Long before the Bible came into its present form, God's people told and retold the sacred stories, making those memories come alive in the hearts of those who listened around the shepherd's campfire or at the well or in the Temple. For generations, the stories of Scripture were passed down from parent to child to grandchild. There was a connection between the present generation and those who had long ago lived their lives in faithfulness. Moses, Deborah, Sarah, and Jacob were not historical figures as much as earlier embodiments of the faithful, each living out God's call to their lives in their own way and time.

In telling our history—whether sharing the sacred story or the tales of the saints in our own congregations—we connect to all of God's people throughout history and to one another as we live in *this* moment of history in our own faithful ways. Rooted in the past, trusting in the future, we are free to act out our faith in the present. Because Moses had such vivid encounters with the Living God, I expect God to be with me in my life-journey. Because Priscilla and Aquila were courageous in telling the Good News of Jesus, I can share *my* faith. Because John Wesley and Mother Teresa dared to evangelize in new ways in out-of-the-way places, I can be creative about my own ministry.

Scripture is not the only aspect of worship that unites us to the past. The place in which we worship is often filled with symbols that remind us of ways God has worked in other places at other times. The empty cross, central in most Christian churches, symbolizes the death and Resurrection of Jesus. Stained-glass windows may tell the biblical story or give testimony to the faith of earlier leaders of our church. Baptismal fonts, banners, and the Lord's Table stand as subtle evocations of our history as God's people. The stoles worn by our pastors and the paraments on the altar are rich in symbols of God's story.

Our liturgy connects us to our history and, as we use contemporary words in our prayer and praise, helps us root ourselves firmly in the present. It is important that we have available the words to historic affirmations of faith such as the Nicene or Apostle's Creed. It is equally crucial that we be able to profess our faith in words familiar to our own experience. Most vital congregations use a balance of the traditional and the contemporary: "How Great Thou Art," "Mah God Is So High," and "God of the Sparrow" telling of God's power; the traditional Lord's Prayer and an inclusive language doxology binding us creatively to tradition.

There should always be a healthy discussion transpiring among the members of a congregation: "Why don't we sing more of the old hymns?" "Why don't we sing more modern music?" "I was really fed by the new sung version of the Lord's Prayer." "I missed saying the 'Our Father.'" Most congregations are composed of a variety of people with different sorts of needs, and all of us grow when we look at our faith from a fresh viewpoint.

For many people, one vital expression of faith is music. Whether we consider ourselves to be of strong voice or not, most of us appreciate the variety of musical interpretations in vital worship: organ or piano pieces, choral anthems, special music by vocal or instrumental soloists, congregational hymns and songs.

Just as music is not static and unchanging, other aspects of worship have changed, too. Our forms of liturgy have moved along with the changes in secular society. Language—a living entity that reflects habits, attitudes, and societal norms—continues to grow and change as well, reminding us to be inclusive of the many varieties of God's people who gather together to worship.

When we use language such as "the community of God," "humanity," and "persons of faith" to describe God's people, we are opening up wider images of those who worship God than if we use the narrower meaning of the generic "men." When we expand our images of God to include "Weaver-woman," "Abba-Inma," "Eagle's Wings," and "Eternal Spirit" as well as "Loving Father," we understand God to be more than our language begins to describe.

These are exciting times as congregations together explore new images and descriptions for God. Some of our traditional ways of looking at the Divine have boxed God into such a narrow description that we have had a limited understanding of God's power and depth. New images help us clarify the mystery of God, even as traditional images sometimes help us feel secure with who we have understood God to be.

We want all worshipers to feel an intimate connection with the God who calls us together. "The use of solely male language for God implies that there is 'common ground' between God and men which does not exist between God and women," writes Marjorie Procter-Smith.[4] The language of our worship should enable and invite all worship participants to know God more personally through Jesus Christ, who reached out to the Samaritan woman and the woman caught in adultery at a time when others considered them lesser beings. Understanding that the language of the Bible is reflective of the times in which it was written, we can look past restrictive

language to the truth expressed by Paul in Galatians 3:28:
"There is no longer Jew or Greek, there is no longer slave or
free, there is no longer male or female; for all of you are one in
Christ Jesus."

The Christian faith must be regenerative, faithful to what
has been and growing into what will be. God's Word, which
has spoken to countless persons since the beginning of time,
will continue to speak to a variety of worshipers. When we
come to worship, open to what God may have to say
specifically to us, we undoubtedly will be touched by the
Spirit of God.

Congregations must find their own balance of traditional
and contemporary because, as Herb Miller reminds us, "If
the worship service is not warm, indigenous, varied, upbeat,
joyful, positive, relational, need-meeting, multi-generation-
al, and live, how can the Christian faith hatch in a new
generation?"[5]

"You know," says Edna Johnson, "all my life I've felt very
comfortable in church. Truth be told, the church of my
childhood was very similar to my adult church." She smiles.
"When worship at my church began to change—different
music, new language, a different order of worship—I was
resistant. 'Why fix it if it isn't broken?' I asked. But now, I find
I have favorite songs in worship that are fairly new to me. And
my concept of God is much bigger now. I have to say that now,
worship means a lot more to me."

Much of our worship experience depends on us—our
life-stage, personality, religious background, the way we feel
on a particular day. If we come to worship fully expecting that
God will speak to us, then we will surely hear some
communication from God. It may come in the Scripture
reading, the sermon, the words of a hymn, or in the glint of
sunlight shining through sanctuary windows.

There are many ways we can prepare ourselves for
corporate worship so that the time actually spent in the

sanctuary is enhanced. For most of us, it is helpful to read the assigned Scripture passages before Sunday morning, letting their words and images rest inside us. Those same words of Scripture that we read silently to ourselves may take on a new meaning when heard in the gathered community.

Our active participation in worship certainly enhances the possibility of our being touched by the service. And the more a worship service speaks to all our senses, the more holistically we can be involved. During the 1988 General Conference of The United Methodist Church in St. Louis, there was a special worship service commemorating the lives of those who had died of AIDS. As worshipers entered the narthex, they were invited to hang a bell on a banner in memory of someone they had known who had died of AIDS. Many of us who were there will always remember the sound of the banner as it was carried down the center aisle at the beginning of the service, bells gently tinkling, reminders of the many gifted individuals whose lives had been all too short. We were touched as well during that service by liturgy, music, dance, and a litany of the names of those who had died. That memorable service touched us in many ways.

We come to worship expecting to meet God. We prepare ourselves inwardly, praying for illumination in our lives. "Help me be open to what the minister has to say this morning, Gracious God. Free my mind from all those things that could easily distract me. Speak to me in this service of worship."

As we have seen, worship is not a performance by the worship leaders for the congregation as audience. Even the sermon time is, in essence, a dialogue. "A sermon is, by definition, a form of speech—a conversation between a preacher and a congregation at a particular time in their lives together, informed by their common worship and reading of scripture," writes Barbara Brown Taylor. "It is a fluid word that is spoken, fluid and warm and transient."[6]

In African-American congregations, the sermon is usually punctuated by verbal affirmations ("Amen," "Preach it!"), which make the sermon more of a dialogue. In many Hispanic churches, worshipers clap at appropriate points in the sermon or wave their bulletins.

Some congregations have as part of their worship service a "talkback" time after the sermon, when members of the congregation have a chance to dialogue more concretely with the sermon. Worshipers may have questions to ask, areas they would like to explore further, or may have their own personal experience to share as part of the illumination process. Out of the dialogue comes greater understanding of the Scripture text as it applies to the real life of the worshipers.

The proclamation of the Word through the sermon can move listeners to respond to God in new and powerful ways. When Peter preached at Pentecost, "those who welcomed his message were baptized, and that day about three thousand persons were added" (Acts 2:41). The effects of such proclamation are not always so immediate or dramatic, however. Many of us require more time to ponder and understand the meaning of a particular sermon and/or Scripture passage for our lives. If there is a specific sermon that you heard in the past and still recall quite clearly, chances are that sermon was and is significant for you in ways you may not fully understand. Sometimes, even sermons which we do not find particularly interesting or eventful at the time we hear them can, years later, strike a chord with our current life experience.

Those of us who hear the Good News of Jesus Christ on a regular basis sometimes become blasé about its impact. We forget that such Good News makes a difference every day of our lives. Today's trials and tribulations (the plant layoffs, our mother-in-law's cancer, more violence in the inner cities) should be seen in the light of the Resurrection.

We forget the drama of the jailer who encountered Paul in a Philippi jail: "He and his entire household rejoiced that he had become a believer in God" (Acts 16:34b). We forget how many people over the centuries have been martyred because they refused to give up faith in Jesus even when they were persecuted for that belief. We forget how many Christians, even today, worship and act out their Christian faith at peril to their lives.

In the last sermon he preached before he was murdered at the death camp of Flossenburg, Dietrich Bonhoeffer spoke on hope, using the Scripture readings for the day: "But he was wounded for our transgressions . . . and by his bruises we are healed" (Isaiah 53:5) and "for whatever is born of God conquers the world. And this is the victory that conquers the world, our faith" (1 John 5:4).[7]

Similarly, Archbishop Oscar Romero was preaching when he was murdered in the chapel of the hospital where he lived. His words responded to Scripture as he said, prophetically, "whoever, out of love for Christ, gives himself to the service of others, will live, like the grain of wheat that dies, but only seems to die. If it did not die, it would remain alone. Only in undoing itself does it produce the harvest."[8]

Even today, a South Korean pastor calling for reunification of North and South Korea is sentenced to five years in jail. People on both sides of the abortion issue are arrested as they respond out of their own understandings of the Christian faith. The Christian faith is not passive or predictable.

We may not be called to martyrdom. But the gospel that is proclaimed in our worship service is calling us to a new understanding of the world and God's power to transform the status quo. And, although we may not immediately know how God will work in us, we do know that we are surrounded by that "great cloud of witnesses," the ones who have gone before us in faith. This includes the women and men of the Bible, those who have lived as Christ's followers in past centuries, the people in our own lives whose faith has touched us, helping us experience God on a deeper level. Grandparents, parents, Sunday school teachers, pastors, and neighbors may have been spiritual guides for us, revealing new layers of God's love to us.

Those of us who live in countries where Christianity is accepted often take for granted the fact that we can worship when, where, and how we please. There are not dramatic moments when we have to stand up tall and shout, "I will worship God and give thanks for my Savior, Jesus Christ!" knowing that those very words may get us in trouble. Yet there may be subtle ways in which we back down on our faith, even as we continue to attend worship and think we are giving praise only to God. Modern society offers insidious temptations that, because they are so much part of mainstream life, seem innocuous.

A recent cinema presentation *Jesus of Montreal* [9] portrayed a powerful scene where Jesus dealt with the reality of contemporary temptation. In the film, a group of actors is asked to put on a modern-day Passion play at a Roman Catholic church. The young man who plays Jesus gives a potent, new interpretation of the Christ-role. One day, a slick media lawyer takes him to the top of a tall building in Montreal to discuss his future. Explaining that the young actor must exploit his talent, define his dreams, and plan steps to achieve them, the well-dressed lawyer says, "Jesus is 'in' these days but you'll have to do the weekend talk shows. . . . There's always more media space than people with things to say. . . . We'll come up with a good script. There are many ways of saying nothing. Radio, television, magazines—you'll be everywhere."

When the young actor does not respond, the lawyer mentions the possibility of publishing a book—"memoirs, travels, your fight against drugs or alcohol, anything. I'm just trying to show you that with your talent, this city is yours if you want it." The camera pulls back to show the two men standing against a window of the skyscraper, the city of Montreal laid out below them in miniature. Suddenly, even before the lawyer continues further, it is obvious. This modern-day Jesus is being tempted just as Satan tempted Jesus in the wilderness.

For us temptations are likely to come even more subtly. There may be times when it seems easier to remain silent rather than to voice our true opinion of a racist joke. It is always easier to keep our faith a private affair, careful not to discuss religion with anyone other than those who belong to our denomination. When faith tells us to jump into the fray of a hot political issue, we may be tempted to stay away from the potential conflict and let others work things out at the school board or in front of the South African Embassy or at a denominational meeting.

In our consumer-oriented society, it is easy to be confused by the values we see so prevalently on television commercials and billboards. "Buy! Buy!" becomes the rallying cry rather than "Live simply so others may simply live." We may also get caught up in societal expectations of who we are supposed to be as men and women, black and white, liberal and conservative, gay and straight. "I am the way, the truth and the life," Jesus said, but all around us are experts on which car to buy, which deodorant to use, where to invest our money, how to make a good first impression.

Into all this confusion, the Word of God walks with confidence. This Word guided the Hebrew people, spoke to the rulers and people of power in many ages, and came softly from the lips of Jesus himself. The Word of God goes beyond time and place and specific social situation. This Word speaks to us whether we live in a tenement building on Chicago's south side or in a Manhattan penthouse. Whether we possess doctorates or are illiterate, this Word can communicate with us.

Communication is a two-way street. We can be open to God's Word as it may come to us in worship. But we also need time alone with the Bible on a regular basis so that the sacred story lives in us. If we have just been reading the story of Shadrach, Meschach, and Abednego, we may feel empowered to stand up for our faith when a co-worker makes a snide remark about the Bible on our desk or the fact that we say grace in the cafeteria. "Be it known to you, O King, that we will not serve your gods and we will not worship the golden statue that you have set up," we hear those three say firmly as they are marched away to the fiery furnace (Daniel 3:18).

Or when certain members of our congregation speak harshly, judging other Christians who they feel don't measure up, we may remember the words of Jesus to his followers: "Do not judge, so that you may not be judged" (Matthew 7:1). When we are feeling afraid, waiting for the results of a cancer biopsy, we feel the comfort of Isaiah 43: "When you pass through the waters, I will be with you; and through the rivers, they shall not overwhelm you; when you walk through fire you shall not be burned, and the flame shall not consume you. . . . Because you are precious in my sight, and honored, and I love you" (verses 2, 4a).

Although the Word of God remains the same as it is printed on a page of a particular translation of the Bible, each time we hear God's Word, we are new people. Because of our experiences from day to day, we hear Scripture with new ears. What is God saying to me *today*? How is the Word of God coming to this congregation at this time?

When the Bible is part of us, *our story* as well as God's, we can face whatever comes to us in life. When we give ourselves to the worship experience wholeheartedly, open to the Spirit that can work in us, we realize that worship is more than a weekly experience. Worship is what we do after we leave the eleven o'clock service as much as how we pray during that service. As one benediction reminds us, "The worship has ended; the service has begun."

Questions for Reflection

— How important is the Bible in my life?
— Do I come to worship open and prepared to encounter God?
— Are there particular verses of Scripture that define my current stage of faith? Have there been sermons that have greatly affected me?
— In my life, what individuals are part of that "great cloud of witnesses" which surrounds and sustains me?

Gathering Around the Table

And we, though many, throughout the earth,
One bread, one body,
one Lord of all,
one cup of blessing which we bless.
And we, though many, throughout the earth,
We are one body in this one Lord.

John B. Foley[1]

F our pairs of hands hold high the broken bread. Four pairs of hands lift chalices into the air, causing nine hundred people to burst into applause at the power of these universal symbols. Once again, the broken bread and poured cup bring good news to the people of God. In this case, it is four white-robed women—three United Methodist bishops and the President-Designate of the British Methodist Church—who preside over the sacred meal for a gathering of United Methodist clergywomen in a hotel "megacenter." It could just as easily be a Liberian priest holding up the communion elements in a city cathedral or a Hispanic lay pastor in southern Texas who offers tortillas and a tray of communion cups to a group of people gathered at a church camp.

Whoever the celebrant, wherever the place, whatever the choice of bread and the fruit of the vine, the Lord's Supper is a time of joy for the Christians who gather to share its nourishment and its meaning. For centuries, Holy Communion has been a time to give praise to God, accept the new life that comes in Christ, and rededicate oneself to the way of Jesus.

If we had been with Jesus on that night when he was betrayed, we might have felt a special celebrative atmosphere. It was Passover and elaborate planning had been made for this meal. Jesus had sent Peter and John to arrange for a room where he and his disciples could observe Passover together in privacy. The disciples had prepared the Passover meal. John tells us that Jesus washed the feet of his disciples, causing at least Peter to feel embarrassed that his Lord would so humble himself.

Jesus used the foot-washing to help the disciples understand what his life and ministry had been about: "If I, your Lord and Teacher, have washed your feet, you also ought to wash one another's feet. For I have set you an example, that you should also do as I have done to you" (John 13:14-15). Jesus was talking about more than the actual act of washing feet. He was speaking of a style of ministry that sought to meet other people's needs rather than to be revered and waited upon. The physical foot-washing demonstrated the symbolic truth of who Jesus was, a serving Lord.

The Gospel of John lifts up this servanthood image as prelude for the meal that is to come. The other three Gospels concentrate on the mealtime during which Jesus used this last time together to summarize what his life on earth had been about.

If we had been there, eating with close friends and a beloved teacher and friend, we might have sensed the import of Jesus' words. Just as likely, however, we might have been so filled with the celebration of Passover and how good it felt simply to be together with people we loved, that we missed the meanings Jesus hoped to impart to his disciples. Don't we often make sense of our life in hindsight? The words spoken by Jesus to those gathered around the table were perhaps not fully understood at that time but, we hope, as the events of the next few days were revealed, Jesus' friends may have begun to grow into the meaning of all that Jesus said.

John gives great detail of Jesus' teaching on that day we now call Maundy (meaning "command") or Holy Thursday. But all the Gospels agree that Jesus told of his impending betrayal. We can only imagine the uproar as each man searched his own heart at the words, "One of you will betray me." Each one present at the Passover table was dealing with his own inner thoughts and feelings even as he tried to keep track of what it was Jesus seemed intent on telling them.

Then, in an action that speaks to us across the centuries, Jesus took common things—a loaf of bread and a cup of wine—and lifted them up with gentle hands. What would we have thought, had we been there with Jesus? Carefully watching him break the bread, receiving our own chunk to eat, how would we have heard the words, "Take, eat; this is my body." And, as we received the cup, feeling the liquid warm our throats, what would it have meant when we heard, "Drink from it, all of you; for this is my blood of the covenant, which is poured out for many for the forgiveness of sins."

Even we who have the perception of time to aid us in understanding realize that in the simplicity of the broken bread and poured-out cup is a complexity of symbol that we may never completely understand. Bread and wine—elements of the earth, simple fare for the hungry—have been transformed into symbols of love, power, and new life. More than physical nourishment, bread and wine become spiritual food, connectors between divine and human.

The Gospels show us how important communal meals were in Jesus' life. Eating with saints and sinners, Jesus shared his thoughts with dinner guests, often giving them more to chew on than the food they were eating. Dinners and banquets were featured in many of his stories, most memorably in the parable of the great feast. When a host invites many people to a great feast, he is angered that they all have excuses for not coming. "Go out at once into the streets and lanes of the town," he tells his servant, "and bring in the poor, the crippled, the blind, and the lame." When that has been done and there is still room at the banquet table, the master orders, "Go out into the roads and lanes, and compel people to come in, so that my house may be filled" (Luke 14:15-24).

In this and other stories, it is clear that God's table is open to all people. At God's table, there are no distinctions of rich or poor, known or unknown, worthy or unworthy. God's love is enough to embrace all people if they but accept the invitation and come to the banquet.

Communion represents that banquet, that chance to feast with all our brothers and sisters. Holy Communion is the center of our congregational life; when we share the bread and the cup, we are bound together in a way that doesn't always happen in other times of worship, study, or fellowship. Paul explained this phenomenon this way: "The cup of blessing that we bless, is it not a sharing in the blood of Christ? The bread that we break, is it not a sharing in the body of Christ? Because there is one bread, we who are many are one body, for we all partake of the one bread" (1 Corinthians 10:16-17).

In our depths, we knew we were united. Somehow, however, in our finance committee meetings and the morning's announcements and that conflict over the color of the new hymnals, we had forgotten. We who are many are one body. Whatever differences we may have brought into worship with us, they are of little consequence now. God calls us to work things out with sisters and brothers before bringing

our gifts to the altar (Matthew 5:23-24), and somehow, the
Lord's Table can be part of that working things out. The
simple act of taking communion encourages us to make an
effort to hear another's point of view and work for
reconciliation.

At this table, this banquet, we stand equal before the God
who loves us. There are no favorite children. Whether we are
at communion for the first or the five-hundredth time, we
stand in the presence of Jesus who said, "Do this in
remembrance of me." And, remembering, we are brought
closer not only to the power of the Risen Christ but to one
another, as well. Christ is our unity. One with him, we are one
with each other. At the table, we feel again the presence of
that "great cloud of witnesses" and know ourselves to be
joined as well to Christians around the globe with whom we
receive these simple symbols of love and forgiveness.

Were we to go to a Christian church on communion Sunday
in Malaysia, Uraguay, Yugoslavia, or Finland, we would find
ourselves being served some form of bread and wine. The
service might feel different, the language might be unknown
to us, but we would know ourselves to be at home. The table
would be spread for all of God's children and we, as different
as we might feel from those with whom we worshiped, would
realize that we were among family, sharing dinner.

Our presence before the Lord's Table means that we are
ready once again to commit ourselves to the One who
willingly died for us. We choose to be faithful and thus, are
one with Jesus as we eat the bread, drink from the cup.

For many of us, as we prepare ourselves to take the bread
and cup, it is a time of looking inward. As Paul wrote to the
church at Corinth, "Examine yourselves, and only then eat of
the bread and drink of the cup" (1 Corinthians 11:28). What
does it mean in *my* life *today* that Jesus gave himself for me?
How does this change my life? We may take a few moments
before or after receiving communion to take stock of our-

selves. There may be a confession time—Am I living up to my
baptismal vows?—and a time of recommitment—How can I
show Christ to the world?

Communion, writes Gustavo Gutiérrez,

> was and can be a revolutionary ritual, one is which we act out
> our faith that the future of God shapes the past and present. "It
> is not a simple memorial. It is not confined to the past, a sort of
> sorrowful and nostalgic recollection of the Lord. It is openness
> to the future, full of trust and gladness."[2]

We are made new, empowered toward the future.

We may pray for the world, especially thinking of its
brokenness and pain. This is my body *broken* for you; this is
my blood *poured out* for you. Where do we see evidence of
that broken body? That poured-out blood? How are we called
to be in solidarity with God's children whose blood is literally
being shed in struggles for liberation? How can we be those
who work to mend the brokenness of militarism or racism?
Remembering Jesus, who gave his all and held back nothing,
the time of communion can be a time of personal
self-evaluation and rededication.

As the communion elements are brought forward with the
offering, we can see clearly the connection between what God
has done, is doing, and will do in and through us. The bread
and cup are offered at the same time that we offer our lives,
ready to work with God in the redemption of the world.

The bread and juice are tangible reminders of God working
in everyday life. Chewing the bread, I am connected with the
earth and its bounty. Swallowing the juice, I give thanks for
the many ways God feeds me. And, like those who walked
with Jesus on the road to Emmaus, my eyes are opened and I
recognize Christ in the breaking of the bread.

Given what a powerful experience Holy Communion can
be in our lives, it may seem ironic that many churches do not

frequently serve the Holy Meal. This pattern is changing in most Protestant churches, and communion, rather than being served quarterly or yearly, is most often a monthly event. Many churches have a weekly communion service in addition to other worship services that serve the Lord's Supper less frequently.

Congregations continue to find new and creative ways in which to serve the Holy Meal. Some still use individual cups of juice and tiny wafers, but more congregations now use loaves of bread and a common chalice for intinction (dipping). Although some churches use only unleavened bread (to signify the manna in the desert given to the Hebrew people), many churches use a variety of breads and different kinds of grape juice or wine. Participants can stand in a circle or in the shape of a cross, serving the bread and cup to each other. Small groups from the congregation may gather around the communion table. Or those receiving the elements can stand in a line, coming forth to receive the bread and cup from pastors or laypeople.

There are many different liturgies for the Holy Meal, but most congregations include the traditional elements of an Invitation, the Great Thanksgiving, the Breaking of the Bread, the Distribution of the Elements. Whether the service is done in a sanctuary, outdoors, or in a home, we retell the story of that last night in Jesus' life and then participate in the meal together, remembering that "Christ has died, Christ has risen, Christ will come again."

Doreen attended her church for several years before she took communion or professed her faith in church membership. A survivor of incest, she had no intention of forgiving her father, so couldn't honestly come to the table in a spirit of total love. Through the help of an incest survivor's group, Doreen was finally able to reach a point where she could let go of past wounds. "I forgive my father," she told the congregation. "I will never be the same because of what he did to me. And I am not willing to relate to him as family. But I have turned all my hurt over to God now. And, as symbol of this new start in my life, I want to join this church and come to the table with you, my family in Christ."

Everett felt alienated from the church for many years because he is gay, and he found the church to be an inhospitable place for people like himself. When he was diagnosed HIV-positive, he felt outright hostility toward religion, especially after he heard a television preacher talk about AIDS as "God's judgment on homosexuals." When a friend talked him into attending a retreat for people with HIV/AIDS, he went cautiously. To his surprise, though, Everett felt at the retreat an unconditional love that included his whole self, virus and all. By the end of the retreat, Everett felt reconnected to God and eagerly joined in when the Lord's Supper was served. "I have missed this," he said. "The bread, the juice—it feels like coming home again."

Maria attends the early service, which features the Lord's Supper, at her church each Sunday because she feels the need to receive the sacrament of Communion on a weekly basis. "Each week, as I stand with my hands cupped ready to receive the bread, I feel as if new life will be poured into me. I like to wait to eat breakfast until after the early service; somehow, when the first food my mouth tastes is the bread and juice, it is a more powerful reminder of how God fills my life."

Doreen, Everett, and Maria knew that they would find healing and strength in the Lord's Supper. They cannot explain what happens in the ritual taking of bread and cup. They know that there is no magical salvation that comes at the moment of communion. Instead, communion reminds them of the gift of salvation that is already theirs. When they come to eat the bread and drink from the cup, past hurts are no longer so important. When they are told, "Do this in remembrance of me," they are empowered to go from the table and share Christ's love.

The everyday symbols of bread and cup nurture us because, in their ordinariness, we know that our ordinary lives are important and connect to God. And since these symbols stand for more than just grain and fruit of the earth, we are fed spiritually as well as physically.

"Holy Communion is the center of congregational life. Through it the people become a congregation united in one body as the body of Christ in the world, fed as one people in order to offer the bread of life to the world."[3] Across the centuries, across the miles, across divisions of nation and class and language, the people of God come together for this holy meal. Sharing the bread and the cup, we know ourselves to be united in Christ Jesus. Whatever other realities may seem apparent, this unity is the prevailing reality.

We come to God's table, eat, and go forth made new, giving thanks for the one bread, one body.

Questions for Reflection

— How do you understand the image of servanthood as Jesus illustrates it in the washing of the disciples' feet?
— What have been some of your most meaningful communion experiences?
— In what ways do you see Jesus' body broken and blood poured out for the world today?
— What does "Christ has died, Christ has risen, Christ will come again" mean in your life?

Living Toward God's New Creation

*Your business now is to stop war, to purify the world, to
get it saved from poverty and riches, to make people like
each other, to comfort the sad, to wake up those who
have not yet found God, to create joy and beauty
wherever you go, to find God in everything and
everyone!*

Muriel Lester

S ome Chicago-area churches celebrate Easter Sunday
together on the shores of Lake Michigan. The congregation gathers in the early morning before the sun is up. The
sound of the water lapping onto the beach reminds them of
the stillness that surely existed as those gathered around the
cross realized that Jesus of Nazareth was dead. When the
service begins, the silence of the Crucifixion is replaced by
the joy of the Resurrection.

He is not dead! He is risen just as he said. And, joyful at the
good news, the worshipers begin to dance. The sun is by now
rising in the sky, its rays shining on the lake. The first kite goes
up, then the second and the third. Symbolizing new life in

Christ, the kites burst into the sky on the wind's wings, reminding all who worship that their faith is not earthbound.

When the Easter congregation leaves the sunrise service, some persons continue to fly kites, others take a walk on the beach, others make their way home. The message is clear: The Resurrected Christ calls us beyond the safe and familiar sanctuaries in which we worship, beyond even the lakeshore where we may feel at home. The Resurrected Christ gives us the freedom to fly as free as kites at the same time that he calls us to go to unknown places. The kite does not know where it will fly but trusts itself to the power of the wind.

"The wind blows where it chooses, and you hear the sound of it," Jesus told Nicodemus, "but you do not know where it comes from or where it goes. So it is with everyone who is born of the Spirit" (John 3:8). As people of the Spirit, we promise to bring new life wherever it is needed. Our work as God's people may take us to Wall Street, public housing, or a base community in Nicaragua. We may find ourselves involved in a bereavement support group, shelter for the homeless, high school Bible study, or prayer group.

Christians have always found ways to act out their faith. Even in the early days, Jesus' followers worshiped together and, by combining their resources, were able to minister to the greater community. Herb Miller reminds us, "New Testament Christians engaged in five activities: worship, learning, fellowship, witnessing, and service. Each of the last four derives its motivational energy from worship."[1]

When we worship, we come to connect with the God who has acted and will continue to act in our lives. Knowing ourselves to be loved and accepted, we feel assured that God can make a difference in our lives. Jesus Christ does indeed bring hope for our future. As we read in Revelation 21:1a, 3-4:

> Then I saw a new heaven and a new earth. . . . I heard a
> loud voice speaking from the throne: "Now God's home is

with humanity! God will live with them, and they shall be God's people. God will be with them, and God will be their God. God will wipe away all tears from their eyes. There will be no more death, no more grief or crying or pain. The old things have disappeared." (AP)

In faith, we live toward that vision. Worship is one way we begin to live toward God's New Creation. We are called to "conversion, to a new way of looking at the world, to a turning around of all [our] accustomed patterns of thinking and living."[2]

Worship reminds us of the past and presents us with a vision for the future. When we worship, we come together in community and are sent into the world ready to work toward God's New Creation. "After my wife died, I was lost," says Franklin Pierce. "My pastor suggested I get involved with our church nursery school. At first, I was hesitant. I have no grandchildren; what did I know about kids? Why did they need *me*? Then, one Sunday, the Scripture lesson said that the greatest in God's realm is one who becomes like a child. 'Whoever welcomes in my name a child like this welcomes me,' it said. And I knew that my work in the nursery school could be a way of welcoming Christ."

Marta Gomez says that a sermon on sexual abuse started her thinking of ways she could make a difference. "I was outraged when I heard the statistics. And when we sang, 'The Voice of God Is Calling,' I was sure I was meant to do whatever I could." Marta now volunteers one day a week at a shelter for abused women in her area.

Faith Church serves a border community. The members were quite aware of the prejudice and misunderstanding that existed between town citizens and those who came across the border in search of a new start in life. After much discussion, Faith Church established El Centro de Amistad at their facility. Remembering that God had told the Israelites,

"Do not deprive foreigners and orphans of their
rights. . . . Remember that you were slaves in Egypt and that
the Lord your God set you free" (Deuteronomy 24:17a, 18
AP). Faith Church people work to help newcomers feel at
home and connect with those who already live in their town.

Jeen Shoung Kim so appreciated the men's Bible study at
his church, he talked to officials at the nearby juvenile home
and started a weekly Bible class for troubled youth. "Surely, I
thought, the Word of God might help these boys turn their
lives around before they get into worse and worse trouble."

Worship opens us up to the variety of needs in our
community and the world. Empowered by God's Spirit, we
share a vision of the world as God intended it. "In recalling
who God is and who we are, we identify the world to itself as
what it yet shall be under the reign of God. It is truly a song for
the beloved sounded back to its Source in the life of God by
creatures who have ears to hear," writes Don Saliers.[3]

How do we sing that love song to God? How can our
congregations be so vital that many will want to join us as we
sing? How do we encourage the world to grow into the "new
earth" that we know is possible?

First, we need to be willing to let go of the things of the
past. The God who says, "See, I am making all things new"
may call us to patterns and practices in worship that are
different than those to which we are accustomed. Being
open to God's Spirit may mean willingness to break old
"rules" that, implicitly or explicitly, have governed our
understandings of worship. Are we accepting of small
children who wave to us and yell at parents as they stand at
the front of the sanctuary during Children's Word? Can we
see the blessing of the youth group's contemporary parable
of the sheep and the goats, even if their choice of music is
offensive to us? Can we let ourselves relax to enjoy an
outdoor worship experience where we are asked to skip in a
circle and shout "Hallelujah!"?

Rather than worrying about whether it is correct or not to clap after an anthem, can we focus on the ways God's Spirit comes to us in the choir's offering? Instead of reading a new hymn and feeling distressed about its new images for God, can we open ourselves to the power of a "Strong Mother God"?

As we begin to let go of past understandings of worship, we are ready to experiment, open to how the Spirit may revitalize our time together in worship. "I grew up at a time when we were not made to feel comfortable with our bodies," says Angie Hartwell. "So when the young adults at our church formed a liturgical dance group, I couldn't imagine why we would want to see them parading their bodies in front of us. I guess I just didn't know how touched I would be to see the prodigal son story danced at the front of the chancel. The meaning of that story came alive for me as never before."

Jayne Burns recalls how she felt when her congregation first tried extended periods of silence in worship. "Boy, was I easily distracted," she remembers. "It seemed like the silence rang out with stomachs growling and rustling papers and coughs. Two minutes of silence at confession time seemed to last forever. Now, I look forward to those minutes of silence, because I know that there are times when the mystery of God takes our words away."

Darrell Zepin says, "When our pastor first started preaching away from the pulpit, I felt ill at ease. I liked having her up where we all could see her. But I soon realized that her presence closer to the congregation made her preaching more intimate. I feel she connects with us in a different way than she did when she was behind that big piece of wood."

Most of us have strong feelings about our sanctuary—where we sit, what the distance is between us and the worship leaders, who our neighbors in the congregation are. When there is a change in our worship space, we often need time to adjust. Does the arrangement of our sanctuary promote interaction between all the actors in worship? Or are we divided into leaders and congregation in a way that does not remind us that we are all acting in praise of God?

The pastor of a new church says, "We consciously chose to have unbolted chairs instead of pews in our sanctuary. It has been a real eye-opener for us to find that when we rearrange our worship space, we have a new perspective on worship itself. For certain church seasons, we place the baptismal font at the entrance to the sanctuary space with the communion table in the middle, surrounded by a congregation in the round. We can also sit in a hexagon or put the communion table at the front as our focus. Rearranging the furniture provides us with new ways to experience God, one another, and how we worship together."

A layperson from another church says, "I love it when we serve communion to one another standing in a circle. Love is made more real to me when I can see the faces of those with whom I am at table. But even when we each walk up to the front of the church to receive communion, I can see who is there, my sisters and brothers in Christ."

Besides being open to new ways of worship, vital congregations involve laypeople, clergy, musicians, and other staff people in the planning and leading of worship. This may take the form of a weekly Bible study group that meets with the pastor to focus on the lectionary passages for the week to come, thereby informing the preacher of their experiences and understandings of those scriptures. Or there may be a worship planning group that, after careful study of the Scripture passages, writes liturgy and chooses hymns for the Sunday worship service.

Other congregations encourage various groups within the church (the youth, women's and men's groups, Sunday school program, Wednesday Bible study) to occasionally take responsibility for the planning and leadership of a Sunday service. This increases the feeling that worship is a shared experience for which all participants are responsible.

> When worship is viewed by the congregation as their work, a great burden is lifted from liturgy leaders. They no longer have to be entertainers or professional inspirers; instead, they do their best to lead everyone in good liturgy work. Without being helped to worship in a personal way, many people turn to other sources to satisfy their hunger. They must be helped to see Christian worship as active participation that demands both discipline and individual freedom, as does all great work.[4]

This sharing of worship planning and leadership is only possible when the appointed clergy as well as laypeople understand the benefit to everyone of sharing responsibility for worship. Different people bring different gifts; a seminary education, music conservatory training, and life experience as a carpenter or registered nurse can all add to the richness of worshiping together.

When worship is seen as a mutual effort, then ministry outside of worship can also be more of a team effort. Paid staff at a church are seen as the facilitators for the congregation's ministry, not the hired hands to represent the congregation.

> We will walk with each other.
> We will walk hand in hand.
> And together, we'll spread the news
> that God is in our land.[5]

Vital worship helps us probe many aspects of ourselves—heart, soul, mind, body. There is a balance of individual meditation and corporate sharing; we have a feeling of the community with which we gather and the world community into which we are called to "go and make of all disciples." When worship is alive and stimulating, we are empowered to go from the worship experience into the world, ready to live toward God's New Creation. Adolfo Pérez Esquivel, in his Nobel Peace Prize acceptance, outlined our task:

Because of our faith in Christ and in humankind, we must apply our humble efforts to the construction of a more just and humane world. And I want to declare emphatically: SUCH A WORLD IS POSSIBLE. To create this new society we must present outstretched, friendly hands, without hatred, without rancor—even as we show great determination, never wavering in the defense of truth and justice. Because we know that seeds are not sown with clenched fists. TO SOW WE MUST OPEN OUR HANDS.[6]

For Franklin Pierce, working for such a new society means being an adopted grandpa at his church nursery school. Marta Gomez found her ministry at a shelter for abused women. Faith Church reached out through its Centro de Amistad. Jeen Shoung Kim offers himself through a Bible class at a juvenile hall. Each individual, each vital congregation lives out the vision of God's New Creation in its own way, sustained by worship experiences that spell out the "new heaven and the new earth" to which God calls us.

> For I am about to create new heavens
>   and a new earth;
> the former things shall not be remembered
>   or come to mind.
> But be glad and rejoice forever
>   in what I am creating;
> for I am about to create Jerusalem as a joy,
>   and its people as a delight. (Isaiah 65:17-18)

With that vision of a place so peaceful that wolves and lambs eat together and there is nothing harmful or evil, we look at our actual world with realistic lenses: How is our world *not* living up to the vision? And also, with the lenses of faith that help us to know that, with God all things are possible.

Worship helps us feel the strength of God's power and our

own capacity to make a difference in the world. Reinhold Niebuhr makes our task easier to tackle when he reminds us that:

> Nothing worth doing is completed in our lifetime, therefore we must be saved by hope. Nothing true or beautiful makes complete sense in any context of history, therefore, we must be saved by faith. Nothing we do, no matter how virtuous, can beaccomplished alone, therefore we are saved by love.[7]

We need hope, faith, and love if we are to be agents of change in this world. We need our community of faith with whom we worship, pray, study, witness, serve. We need to remember that "I am with you always, to the end of the age."

Sustained by God, redeemed by Christ, nourished by the Spirit, we go forth from worship ready to live into God's New Creation.

Questions for Reflection

— How does my worshiping community reflect God's New Creation?

— Does worship challenge me to work toward a new reality, or do I feel comfortable in the status quo?

— How has worship sent me forth into my specific ministry?

— When I think of the "new heaven and new earth," what images come to mind?

1. Connecting to God

1. Annie Dillard, *Holy the Firm* (New York: Harper Colophon, 1977), p. 55.
2. Abraham Joshua Heschel, *I Asked for Wonder* (New York: Crossroad Press, 1987), p. 3.
3. Joe Elmore and Kay Mutert, *Songs for the Journey* (Birmingham: Songs for the Journey), p. 57.
4. Brother Lawrence, *The Practice of the Presence of God,* trans. Robert J. Edmonson (Orleans, Mass.: Paraclete Press, 1985), p. 145.
5. Tennessee Williams, *A Streetcar Named Desire* (New York: New Directions Books, 1947), p. 116.
6. Brother Lawrence, *The Practice of the Presence of God,* p. 55.
7. Kahlil Gibran, *The Prophet* (New York: Alfred A. Knopf, 1923), pp. 77-78.

2. Gathering with Other Believers

1. In *Touch Holiness: Resources for Worship,* ed. Ruth C. Duck and Maren C. Tirabassi (New York: Pilgrim Press, 1990), p. 211.
2. *Worship at Campus Chapel,* a brochure of the Christian Reformed campus ministry at the University of Michigan.

3. William Willimon, *Why I Am a United Methodist* (Nashville: Abingdon Press, 1990), p. 58.

4. John Woolman, *The Journal and Essays of John Woolman*, ed. Amelia Mott Gunmore (Philadelphia: Friends Bookstore, 1922).

5. James White, as quoted in Linda Clark, Marian Ronan, and Eleanor Walker, *Image Breaking/Image Building: A Handbook for Creative Worship with Women of the Christian Tradition* (New York: Pilgrim Press, 1981), p. 11.

6. Don E. Saliers, *Worship and Spirituality* (Philadelphia: Westminster Press, 1984), p. 36.

7. Søren Kierkegaard, *The Purity of Heart Is to Will One Thing* (New York: Harper & Row, 1967), p. 181.

8. David G. Owen, *Transparent Worship* (New York: Women's Division, Board of Global Ministries of The United Methodist Church, 1973), p. 14.

3. Building Community

1. In *Touch Holiness: Resources for Worship*, ed. Ruth C. Duck and Maren C. Tirabassi (New York: Pilgrim Press, 1990), p. 173.

2. Dietrich Bonhoeffer, *Life Together* (London: SCM Press, 1972), p. 15.

3. Henri J. M. Nouwen, *The Genesee Diary: Report from a Trappist Monastery* (Garden City, N.Y.: Doubleday, 1976), p. 139.

4. Sheila Cassidy, *Prayer for Pilgrims: A Book About Prayer for Ordinary People* (New York: Crossroads Press, 1982), pp. 4-5.

5. In *Touch Holiness: Resources for Worship*, ed. Duck and Tirabassi, p. 176.

6. John H. Westerhoff III, in ibid., pp. 55, 57.

4. Understanding Our Place in God's World

1. Abraham Joshua Heschel, *I Asked for Wonder: A Spiritual Anthology*, ed. Samuel H. Dresner (New York: Crossroads Press, 1987), p. 20.

2. John H. Westerhoff III, *Living the Faith Community: The Church That Makes a Difference* (Minneapolis: Winston Press, 1985), p. 47.

3. David Owen, *Transparent Worship* (New York: Women's Division, Board of Global Ministries of The United Methodist Church, 1973), p. 22.

4. *Awakenings*, a Columbia picture, screenplay by Steve Zaillian from the book by Oliver Sack, M.D.

5. Kenneth Bedell, *Worship in the Methodist Tradition* (Nashville: Discipleship Resources/Tidings, 1976), p. 3.

5. Living into the Word of God

1. In *Touch Holiness: Resources for Worship*, ed. Ruth C. Duck and Maren C. Tirabassi (New York: Pilgrim Press, 1990), p. 210.
2. William Willimon, *With Glad and Generous Hearts: A Personal Look at Sunday Worship* (Nashville: The Upper Room, 1986), p. 79.
3. Don Saliers, *Worship and Spirituality* (Philadelphia: Westminster Press, 1984), pp. 17-18.
4. Marjorie Procter-Smith, *In Her Own Rite: Constructing Feminist Liturgical Tradition* (Nashville: Abingdon Press, 1990), p. 62.
5. Herb Miller, *How to Build a Magnetic Church* (Nashville: Abingdon Press, 1987), p. 56.
6. Barbara Brown Taylor, *Mixed Blessings* (Marrietta, Ga.: Cherokee, 1986) as reviewed in *Weavings* (July/August 1989), p. 43.
7. Mary Craig, *Candles in the Dark: Six Modern Martyrs* (London: Hodder and Stoughton, 1984), p. 54.
8. Ibid., p. 204.
9. *Jesus of Montreal*, Max Films Productions, 1990, produced by Denys Arcand.

6. Gathering Around the Table

1. John B. Foley, "One Bread, One Body," copyright © 1978, 1989 by John B. Foley, S.J., and New Dwn Music, P.O. Box 13248, Portland, OR 97213-0248. All rights reserved. Used by permission.
2. Gustavo Gutiérrez, as quoted in Paul G. King, Kent Maynard, and David O. Woodyard, *Risking Liberation: Middle Class Powerlessness and Social Heroism* (Atlanta: John Knox Press, 1988), p. 169.
3. The Council of Bishops of The United Methodist Church, *Vital Congregations—Faithful Disciples: A Vision for the Church* (Nashville: Graded Press, 1990), pp. 135-36.

7. Living Toward God's New Creation

1. Herb Miller, *How to Build a Magnetic Church* (Nashville: Abingdon Press, 1987), p. 56.
2. The Council of Bishops of The United Methodist Church, *Vital Congregations—Faithful Disciples* (Nashville: Graded Press, 1990), p. 115.

3. Don E. Saliers, *Worship and Spirituality* (Philadelphia: Westminster Press, 1984), p. 40.
4. Thomas Emswiler and Sharon Neufer Emswiler, *Wholeness in Worship* (San Francisco: Harper & Row, 1980), p. 79.
5. Peter Scholtes, "They'll Know We Are Christians by Our Love," F.E.L. Publications. Reproduced by permission. Permit No. P01873.
6. Adolfo Pérez Esquivel, December 10, 1980 Nobel Peace Prize acceptance speech.
7. Reinhold Niebuhr, as quoted in Mark J. Link, *In the Stillness Is the Dancing* (Niles, Ill.: Argus Communications, 1972), p. 62.

Alternate Rituals Project. *Ritual in a New Day*. Nashville: Abingdon Press, 1976.

Bedell, Kenneth. *Worship in the Methodist Tradition*. Nashville: Discipleship Resources/Tidings, 1976.

Birch, Bruce C. "Memory in Congregational Life," *Congregations: Their Power To Form and Transform*, ed. by C. Ellis Nelson. Atlanta: John Knox Press, 1988.

Bonhoeffer, Dietrich. *Life Together*. London: SCM Press, 1972.

Callahan, Kennon. *Twelve Keys to an Effective Church*. San Francisco: Harper & Row, 1983.

Cassidy, Sheila. *Prayers for Pilgrims: A Book About Prayer for Ordinary People*. New York: Crossroad, 1982.

Clark, Linda; Ronan, Marian; and Walker, Eleanor. *Image-Breaking/Image-Building: A Handbook for Creative Worship with Women of Christian Tradition*. New York: Pilgrim Press, 1981.

Craig, Mary. *Candles in the Dark: Six Modern Martyrs*. London: Hodder and Stoughton, 1986.

Cummings, Charles. *The Mystery of the Ordinary: The Richness of Everyday Experience*. San Francisco: Harper & Row, 1982.

Dillard, Annie. *Holy the Firm*. New York: Harper Colophon, 1977.

Duck, Ruth C. and Tirabassi, Maren C. *Touch Holiness: Resources for Worship*. New York: Pilgrim Press, 1990.

Edmonson, Robert J., trans. *The Practice of the Presence of God by Brother Lawrence*. Orleans, Mass.: Paraclete Press, 1985.

Foster, Richard J. *Celebration of Discipline: The Path to Spiritual Growth*. San Francisco: Harper & Row, 1978.

Gibran, Kahlil. *The Prophet*. New York: Alfred A. Knopf, 1923.

Hays, Edward. *Prayers for the Domestic Church: A Handbook for Worship in the Home*. Topeka, Kansas: Forest of Peace Books, 1979.

Heschel, Abraham Joshua. *I Asked for Wonder: A Spiritual Anthology* ed. by Samuel H. Dresner. New York: Crossroad, 1987.

Hickman, Hoyt L. *United Methodist Worship*. Nashville: Abingdon Press, 1991.

Killinger, John. *Leave It to the Spirit*. London: SCM Press, 1971.

King, Paul G; Maynard, Kent; and Woodyard, David O., *Risking Liberation: Middle Class Powerlessness and Social Heroism*. Atlanta: John Knox Press, 1988.

Link, Mark J. *In the Stillness Is the Dancing*. Niles, Ill.: Argus Communications, 1972.

Miller, Herb. *How to Build a Magnetic Church*. Nashville: Abingdon Press, 1987.

Neufer Emswiler, Thomas and Sharon. *Wholeness in Worship: Creative Models for Sunday, Family, and Special Services*. San Francisco: Harper & Row, 1980.

Nouwen, Henri J. M., *The Genesee Diary: Report from a Trappist Monastery*. Garden City, N.Y.: Doubleday and Company, 1976.

Owen, David G. *Transparent Worship*. New York: Women's Division, Board of Global Ministries, 1973.

Procter-Smith, Marjorie. *In Her Own Rite: Constructing Feminist Liturgical Tradition*. Nashville: Abingdon Press, 1990.

Saliers, Don E. *Worship and Spirituality*. Philadelphia: Westminster Press, 1984.

Steere, Douglas V. *Prayer and Worship*. Richmond, Ind.: Friends United Press, 1978.

The United Methodist Council of Bishops. *Vital Congregations Faithful Disciples: Vision for the Church*. Nashville: Graded Press, 1990.

Westerhoff, John H., III. *Living the Faith Community: The Church That Makes a Difference*. Minneapolis: Winston Press, 1985.

Williams, Tennessee. *A Streetcar Named Desire*. New York: New Directions Books, 1947.

Willimon, William H. *Remember Who You Are: Baptism, a Model for Christian Life*. Nashville: The Upper Room, 1980.

———. *Why I Am a United Methodist*. Nashville: Abingdon Press, 1990.

———. *With Glad and Generous Hearts: A Personal Look at Sunday Worship*. Nashville: The Upper Room, 1986.

Winter, Miriam Therese. *Woman Prayer Woman Song: Resources for Ritual*. Oak Park, Ill.: Meyer Stone Books, 1987.